THE SCREAM QUEEN'S SURVIVAL GUIDE

STARRING MEREDITH O'HAYRE

AVOID MACHETES, DEFEAT EVIL CHILDREN,
STEER CLEAR OF BLOODY DISMEMBERMENT,
AND CONQUER OTHER HORROR MOVIE CLICHÉS

Aadamsmedia
Avon, Massachusetts

Published by
Adams Media, a division of F+W Media, Inc.
57 Littlefield Street, Avon, MA 02322. U.S.A.
www.adamsmedia.com

ISBN 10: 1-4405-0609-4
ISBN 13: 978-1-4405-0609-3
eISBN 10: 1-4405-0864-X
eISBN 13: 978-1-4405-0864-6

Printed in the United States of America.

10   9   8   7   6   5   4   3   2   1

Library of Congress Cataloging-in-Publication Data
O'Hayre, Meredith.
The scream queen's survival guide : avoid machetes, defeat evil children,
steer clear of bloody dismemberment, and conquer other horror movie
clichés / Meredith O'Hayre.
p. cm.
Includes index.
ISBN 978-1-4405-0609-3 (alk. paper)
1. Horror films—History and criticism. 2. Horror films—Humor. I. Title.
PN1995.9.H6O37 2010
791.43'6164—dc22
2010019566

This book is available at quantity discounts for bulk purchases.
For information, please call 1-800-289-0963.

For Doc.
Who is afraid of scary movies—but mows a mean lawn
And, for the most part, lets me control the clicker.

ACKNOWLEDGMENTS

Without the love of my family—both the ones with whom I am lucky enough to share DNA and my unbelievably awesome friends who have become my family over the years—I would not have the confidence to say, "Well, I think I could write a book," and then actually follow through on it. Thank you all for everything.

This book wouldn't have come to fruition without the support of the Adams Media team, particularly Karen Cooper, Phil Sexton, Paula Munier, Wendy Simard, and Sue Beale, and for that support I am extremely grateful.

A HUGE thank you to those who worked on this book and helped to take it from a rough cut to big screen debut: Matt Glazer, who had the great idea for this book and trusted me enough to write it; Katie Corcoran Lytle, who edited it so carefully; Casey Ebert and Skye Alexander, who helped to polish it; Frank Rivera, who created my kick-ass cover and took my author photo; Elisabeth Lariviere, who lent her artistic talent to designing the interior; and Beth Gissinger-Rivera who helped spread the word about my weird little book to the horror-loving masses.

It's true what they say: it takes a village to create a crass, tongue-in-cheek book about scary movies.

Scream Queen (noun): Originating in the 1920s and revived in the late 1970s, primarily due to Jamie Lee Curtis's extensive horror movie résumé, this term refers to the female protagonist in the horror genre.

Unlike the other characters who fall victim to predictable scary movie clichés, these heroines are, most often, the last ones standing.

CONTENTS

PART 4

GIVING A WHOLE NEW MEANING TO THE TERM "BACK STABBERS" 127

PART 5

OH, FREAK OUT! 169

WARNING

In addition to giving you a case of the heebie-jeebies, this book will also give away some key plot points and endings to some of the movies referenced within these pages. If you want to avoid finding out essential plot points and not-so-surprise endings, steer clear of the Spoiler Alerts that are sprinkled throughout this book, which are flagged with a ⚠. Although I only do this in an effort to keep you alive and to fully explain the potential consequences if you don't adhere to these crucial survival tips, that's the bad news.

The good news is that horror movies are entertaining, delightfully creepy, sometimes funny, and always horrifying, but they are not (with some notable exceptions) highly regarded for their shocking endings. There are only so many ways a movie with a meat cleaver as one of the most-often-used props can end.

Consider yourself warned.

Introduction

WHAT WAS YOUR FIRST?

You always remember your first.

You'll never forget the first time you heard the chilling piano music in *Halloween*, alerting you that Michael Myers was about to make an attempt on Laurie's life, yet again. Or the first time you watched Jack Nicholson's psychotic, *Shining* face appear through the newly renovated bathroom door. And definitely not the first time you saw the scared-stiff face of a twenty-something documentarian filming *The Blair Witch Project* as she heard her friends and fellow campers get picked off, one by one.

When it comes to scary movies, the firsts don't end there. What about the first time you watched a chick volunteer to investigate the weird noise in the basement, only to end up sliced and diced? Or the first time you saw a dim-witted damsel use the ol' bureau-against-the-bedroom-door method of keeping a killer at bay—resulting in the same girl being forced to jump out the window to escape the ruthless maniac?

Whether you were ten or seventeen, you undoubtedly recall that feeling of intellectual superiority the first time you slapped your hand against your head and thought to yourself, *Really? This is the best this girl can do?* After all, almost every slasher flick has at least one scene that makes one thing stunningly clear: there are a lot of dumb girls out there.

But for every seven female characters who end up beheaded, burned, and quartered during the course of ninety to one hundred and twenty minutes, there is one survivor: the Scream Queen. This is not to say that attempts to take down the Scream Queen have not been made. At the end of a slasher flick, she has most likely been shot at, stabbed, dragged from a moving car, poisoned, almost-drowned, and the near-victim of many more heinous assaults too vulgar to get into while we're still on the introduction (although trust me—we'll get there). But the Scream Queen prevails. And *The Scream Queen's Survival Guide* is here to tell you how.

Throughout the course of this book, you'll be treated to a lesson in all things kick ass—courtesy of Scream Queens. Using survival techniques employed in hundreds of the most (and least) popular horror flicks of all time, you'll learn how to handle the creepiest of life's situations—ranging from what to do when you think the kid next door might be an undead child from another century to how to handle a telekinetic classmate hell-bent on making you the main course at the prom.

So grab your stake, your promiscuous but likeable best friend, and your uncanny ability to keep your hair perfectly coiffed even when being chased by a murderer—and get ready to learn the ins and outs of surviving the scariest hour and a half of your life from the most resilient character in the history of film: the Scream Queen.

PART 1

A DAY LIKE ANY OTHER

"WE ALL GO A LITTLE MAD SOMETIMES."
—*PSYCHO*

CHAPTER 1

MAKING IT OUT ALIVE

Like every good horror movie, we'll start at the beginning. Just as Miyagi taught Ralph Macchio the art of painting a fence and trimming tiny little trees so that he would one day "Sweep the leg!" so too will I give you a few basics you should pay close attention to—that is, if you want to live to see the sequel.

INVEST IN CALLER ID

THE CALL IS COMING FROM INSIDE THE HOUSE!

It's impossible to know how many lives were unnecessarily snuffed out before the invention of Caller ID. After all, would you ever even answer the phone if it said, "Incoming call from Freaky Little Dead Girl at the Bottom of a Well"?

And there's no doubt Drew Barrymore would have made it past minute six in the first *Scream* movie had she been able to pick up and say, "Hey, asshole in the freaky skull mask—I have your callback number here!" Most of us have been rocking Caller ID since the mid-nineties, but a few Stone-Agers out there refuse to pay extra for this "modern" convenience.

If you (or your parents) are one of the holdouts, consider how much your life is worth. Won't the extra $3.27 a month pay for itself in the long run? Hey, whether you're avoiding telemarketers or a recently-escaped-from-a-mental-institution murderer, you know better than to pick up "Incoming Call: Private Number."

 SCREAM QUEEN SAYS *There are few things more satisfying than sending a serial killer to voicemail.*

KEEP YOUR V-CARD

FOR ONCE, BE THANKFUL YOU'RE A VIRGIN.

This lesson is as old as horror films themselves: the slutty chick or sex-hungry dude dies first.

True, you may get irritated (literally) by limiting your sexual contact to solo bubble baths, but scary movies have taught us that if you get laid in the first scene, you'll be dead by the third. *But everyone dies in these movies!* you think. *If I'm going to die, shouldn't it be with a smile on my face?*

Consider some of the death scenes for characters in slasher flicks who were lucky enough to get a piece before they ate it. Some of them went first, but their deaths are pretty much the worst in the films. (Well, worst for them. Best for us.)

- In the opening minutes of *Halloween,* poor Judith Myers has the misfortune of both having sex with a guy with a bad seventies haircut and a clown mask AND then getting knifed to death by her six-year-old brother while he wears the same mask. Even if she hadn't been murdered, the girl never would have responded well to the circus. Too many conflicting urges: *Do I take my pants off or run for my life?*
- Oli in *Hostel* is beheaded (and God knows what else) within the first twenty minutes of the movie. True, he avoided getting his fingers cut off, but presumably didn't have a pleasant night with his Slovakian hosts.
- In *The Shining,* Jack gets a peek at a beautiful and butt-nekkid lady getting out of the tub. Before he can do anything about this incredible stroke of luck, she turns into a hideous old woman right before his eyes. ⚠ Later that day, he'll end up frozen in a maze. Yes, his fate was of his own making—but this close encounter of the sexual kind surely sped things along. And one can only guess that Jack wanted a more pleasant image to send him to his final, frozen destination. ⚠
- The lure of sex proved to be the downfall for a few of the characters in 2009's *Jennifer's Body.* Thinking they were about to score with the hottest girl in their high school,

jocks and emo kids alike wound up disemboweled and half-eaten. Although they didn't deserve to die, these kids were seriously challenged if they thought someone who looked like Megan Fox would be interesting in robbing them of their virginity.

There's no great lesson here. The bottom line is horror and sex do not mix—so heed the advice of the Scream Queen wisely.

 SCREAM QUEEN SAYS *Keep it in your pants.*

SURVIVAL TIP

JUST SAY NO

A JOINT NEVER HURT ANYONE—IT'S THAT AXE THAT WILL RUIN YOUR NIGHT.

Everyone enjoys a couple (dozen) beers or some old fashioned gravity hits now and again. So who knew the people who make horror movies were such a bunch of stiffs? Apparently, these squares (as your mom would call them) don't care for those who just say "Hell, yes!" In fact, in slasher flicks, the lesson is pretty clear: You drink or get high and you end up beheaded by a monster, as in *Feast*, or hacked to bits and shoved in a closet, as in *Prom Queen*. In fact, it's such a cliché in horror movies that it's long rumored to be a message from the Christian Right.

Yeah, because the Christian Right spends a lot of time working on horror movies.

Although not as much fun as chasing a few tabs of acid with a Miller High Life, sometimes staying sober is the only way to make it through the night without experiencing the unique and indescribable feeling of an axe through your face. So how should you pass the time when there's a serial butcher on the loose and you don't have the option of getting blitzed on Jack? Consider a more natural high. We've all heard the urban legend that says drinking copious amounts of water can make you hallucinate—maybe tonight is the night to find out if it's possible! Or get some cardio in; boosting your endorphins will make it almost impossible for those pesky little casualties to get you down. This will actually benefit you in a couple of ways—your sobriety will help you stay on your toes, rendering you less susceptible to the killer's advances, AND you'll get in shape, increasing both your speed and ability to run away from someone who may want to make you into a skin suit.

 SCREAM QUEEN SAYS *Lay off the sauce.*

NEED PROOF?

Here are just a few of the movies where drinking and/ or drugs led to an early death—and we're not talking overdosing here: *Halloween, Hostel, Urban Legend, The Ring, The Blair Witch Project, The Shining, Jennifer's Body, Jaws, I Know What You Did Last Summer, Shaun of the Dead, The Hand that Rocks the Cradle, The Ruins, The Thing* . . . you get the point.

I need a drink.

STAY ABREAST OF CURRENT EVENTS

POLICE IN ARKANSAS CONTINUE TO BE ON THE LOOKOUT FOR A SAVAGE SERIAL KILLER, LAST SEEN WEARING A UNIVERSITY OF ILLINOIS T-SHIRT AND HOLDING A SIGN THAT READ CHICAGO OR BUST!

One inarguable truth about people in horror movies is this: they're very slow to put two and two together. It's only when one-eyed Pete is standing over them with a meat hook that they remember reading something about a crazed butcher who escaped from a mental institution in the next town and has a vengeance for college students. Or when they're staring down an alien dead set on drinking their brain fluid that they recall thinking to themselves while driving by their neighbor's farm, *I don't remember seeing that crop circle yesterday!*

In the event that your town has recently come under attack, why not stay ahead of the game and tune in to your local and national news to see if anyone or anything suspicious is on the run? That way, you won't be taken by surprise and end up at the bottom of a harbor with an anchor secured to your ankle when The Ankle Anchor Killer comes through your town. Or killed with a two-foot drill like the poor chicks in *The Slumber Party Massacre* who were too busy planning their sleepover to watch the top news story about a disturbed man named Russ Thorn who recently escaped from prison. Bummer for them. If you want to stay one step ahead of the Russ Thorns of the world, switch over to the news every once in a while.

Sound obvious? Of course. But we've seen countless slasher movie characters meet an early demise because they decided to watch the movie of the week (usually, a horror movie) instead of paying attention to an eager anchorwoman's warning that young women with long hair should avoid wearing gray hooded sweatshirts and walking home alone from softball practice between the hours of 8 and 9 P.M. on Tuesdays and Fridays.

 **SCREAM QUEEN SAYS** *Get your head out of your ass.*

TALK ABOUT IGNORING THE *SIGNS*

Perhaps the movie in which the not-so-friendly invaders give the biggest heads-up of all is M. Night Shyamalan's *Signs.* In fact, the tagline for the 2002 film is "It's Not Like They Didn't Warn Us."

In this horror/thriller starring a pre-drunk-driving anti-Semite Mel Gibson and a pre-gone-off-the-deep-end-and-given-up-grooming Joaquin Phoenix, invading aliens do all but call ahead to let the residents of planet Midwest know they're coming. They leave crop circles, communicate through baby monitors—even make an appearance at a South American birthday party that Mel's family catches on the news. All this and Mr. Braveheart is *still* surprised when they arrive.

It kinda makes you wonder . . . what was he waiting for—an e-vite to the invasion?

THINK TWICE ABOUT THAT "BLONDES HAVE MORE FUN" THING

IT DOESN'T MATTER WHAT COLOR YOUR HAIR IS WHEN YOUR HEAD IS NO LONGER ATTACHED TO YOUR BODY!

The tenth commandment of horror movies is: If you're a pretty blonde, you won't see tomorrow.

Perhaps it stems from jealousy of the flaxen-haired. Or the disappointing realization that hot blondes tend to date fellow hot blondes, not moderately disfigured social outcasts who go around killing people. Whatever the reason, the end result is the same—the blonde girl always dies.

It's been proven that blondes receive more compliments on their looks, are served faster in bars, and get more warnings but fewer traffic tickets than the rest of us. However, at some point you must consider just how important that pretty blonde head is to you. You're fairer-than-typical hairdo won't do you any good if your eyes are gouged out and you're put on a stake. When a murderer is on the loose in your tri-state area, your first stop should be the hair color aisle of your local pharmacy. Not convinced? Consider the lineup of blondes killed in horror movies:

- Drew Barrymore as Casey in *Scream*
- Sarah Michelle Gellar as Helen in *I Know What You Did Last Summer*
- Paris Hilton as Paige in *House of Wax*
- P. J. Soles as Lynda van der Klok in *Halloween*
- Alison Lohman as Christine Brown in *Drag Me to Hell*
- Betty Buckley as Miss Collins in *Carrie*

Still not convinced, Blondie? You'll make it too easy for the killer. Don't be a dumb blonde.

 SCREAM QUEEN SAYS *Like most rules, this doesn't apply to you, Paris. We love you as a blonde! Never change.*

SURVIVAL TIP

LOOK A GIFT HORSE IN THE MOUTH

THIS MOST-LIKELY-HAUNTED ANCIENT URN WILL LOOK LOVELY IN MY GUEST BATHROOM. THANK YOU SO MUCH!

Everyone loves getting a gift—the carefully tied bow, the touching sentiment of the accompanying note, the tortured spirit of the original, long-dead owner still attached to the object. Wait, what?

There is an exception to the rule of gift-loving. You will not enjoy a present should you discover after the fact that your acceptance of this gift includes the following:

- an expedited and particularly horrifying death
- a rare but nonetheless irritating illness, the symptoms of which include hallucinations of people hurling themselves off of cliffs, profusive coughing that results in a mouthful of hair, and the particularly annoying problem of insects seemingly appearing out of nowhere and flying out of your nose
- a verbal, written, or spiritual agreement that the gift-giver shall be entitled to the recipient's soul in return

When such generosity occurs in horror films, the result is almost always the same, whether the gift is an ability to turn costume jewelry from Target into Tiffany's finest, or the aforementioned haunted vase: the receiver is tormented, tortured, and emotionally and physically ruined, even if he or she is allowed to live. You see, as with workout DVDs ordered through infomercials, nothing in horror movies is ever really free—and you won't even get the bonus of ripped abs. The giver is almost always looking for something in return.

So how do you ensure you won't end up the unknowing owner of a gift that is guaranteed to mess up your weekend and most likely the rest of your life? Glad you asked.

THE SCREAM QUEEN'S GUIDE TO STAYING AWARE OF GIFTS THAT HOLD THE POTENTIAL TO RUIN YOUR LIFE		
GOOD GIFT	LAME GIFT	GONNA-GET-YOU-KILLED GIFT
A midpriced bottle of Pinot Chard	A $10 Starbucks card	An ancient book of incantations, wrapped in burlap and deposited on your front step
Cute lingerie that makes your stomach look flatter without looking slutty	A coupon for two hours of sexy time	A potion guaranteed to attract the attention of the guy you want—as well as that of undead demons intent on occupying your body so they can carry out their unfinished business of decimating an entire small town
A subscription to Netflix	A gift certificate to Videos 'R Us	A grainy video of a series of unrelated but equally disturbing images filmed by a young dead girl stuck in the bottom of a well

Still worried that you'll have trouble IDing a gift that could end up ending your life? Just politely say, "No thanks!" the next time you're offered a gift by someone who is dead, a messenger for the dead, fascinated with death, or otherwise involved in the business of death. This includes little pale girls who run on all fours, serial killers reiterating the importance of the Seven Deadly Sins through appropriately themed murders, and gypsies you hit with your car.

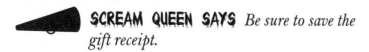 **SCREAM QUEEN SAYS** *Be sure to save the gift receipt.*

BE WARY OF DAYS THAT BEGIN MUCH LIKE ANY OTHER

THE RESIDENTS OF THIS SLEEPY LITTLE TOWN HAD NO IDEA WHAT WAS IN STORE FOR THEM . . .

Very few horror movies start with heads rolling. Sure, there are the *Saws* and the *Jaws* in which blood flows even before the opening credits have rolled. But for the most part, slasher flicks all start the same way—with a day like any other.

Often, we see our Scream Queen going about her daily business—whether that is going to school, running errands, or getting ready for the senior prom. After pausing to stare at a picture of her dead parents, she continues on her way, none the wiser that things are about to take a turn for the way, way worse.

How the hell, I can hear you thinking, *am I supposed to keep an eye out for things being too normal?* Take a lesson from the residents of the Town Like Any Other in countless horror movies and be on the lookout for:

- A shadowy figure in the bushes, holding a picture of you from a local newspaper article about your family's tragic and unsolved murder

- Your hometown looking excessively bright and friendly, punctuated by neighbors and townspeople who greet you by name as you make your way through the quaint downtown
- Any news stories about an escaped mental patient who may be on the loose in your area
- A local police officer who seems particularly interested in your plans for the weekend
- Creepy instrumental music that follows you wherever you go
- A particularly sunny day with the weather station calling for an impending storm, flood, and possible evacuations

I hate to be a Debbie Downer here, but be on the lookout when things start to really look up. It's the perfect time for Mother Nature, an escaped psychopath, or a deranged officer of the law to swoop in and take a giant shit on your life. So if things seem to be going too well in Small Quaint Town, keep an eye out for things that appear ordinary in the extreme. You'd hate to miss a beautiful Saturday because you're chained up in somebody's basement.

 SCREAM QUEEN SAYS *When things seem too good to be true, it's not usually because you're about to friggin' die. But better safe than sorry.*

SURVIVAL TIP

REFRAIN FROM HYPERBOLE

THIS IS GOING TO BE THE BEST NIGHT EVER!

In and of itself, excitement is a good thing. Anticipation over the little stuff (the possibility of winning a couple bucks on a scratch ticket, the Chinese food delivery guy remembering to give you extra-spicy mustard for the first time ever) to the big (high school graduation, your first night in a new house) is what makes everyday life a bit more exhilarating. But in a slasher flick, there's no surer way to get yourself killed than to indulge in a bit of hyperbole. So think twice before you allow yourself to get all piss-your-panties psyched.

When it comes to surviving a horror movie, it's best to shoot for the middle. Think about it, almost every horror movie starts with the promise of something amazing: a group of friends heads out for an awesome camping weekend, two girlfriends embark on an unforgettable road trip, a group of seniors get ready for the best prom night ever, a couple flies to an exotic locale for a romantic weekend, a bright-eyed and promising young girl heads to college with dreams for the future.

When you're *whoo-hooooooo*ing out of the sunroof of a limo or packing your bag to head to Tahiti, it's hard to keep your excitement in check. But before you scream, "I love everyone!" or tell your boyfriend you have a feeling, "This is going to be the best vacation we've ever taken," think back on how it always goes in the horror movies: the best weekend/night/vacation/prom turns out to be the same one where everyone in attendance is chopped into little bits and stuffed into a hotel janitor closet/storage unit/industrial-sized cooler/senior class time capsule. And shit usually goes down right after someone declares that that night/day/vacation/dance is going to be the best ever.

This shouldn't come as a surprise to anyone who knows scary movies, but serial killers, psychopaths, and mental defectives in general don't get much pleasure from other people's happiness. Their biz is generally misery and torture. After all, ruthless killers rarely come from happy, well-adjusted families—and they NEVER have happy high school years. So while you should by all means enjoy yourself on your senior class trip to the amusement park or girls' weekend in Vegas, keep your joy to yourself. You just never know when someone with homicidal tendencies is watching as you toast to the best night ever.

 SCREAM QUEEN SAYS *It's your best head ever, too, so try to keep it.*

SURVIVAL TIP

WATCH YOUR FUCKING MOUTH, ASSHOLE

WHAT THE ##$! IS THIS #@$!ING #$^$ ABOUT, MOTHER$%&*#$?

Swearing while there's a murderer on the loose? You're fucking nuts.

This comes down to an issue of ratings. As in "R" for "restricted." Any horror movie worth its mustard earns itself a rating of R. It's hard to sneak beheadings, disembowelments, and ritualistic torture past the Motion Picture Association of America. And once you're into the R rating, not only do the limbs start flying, so do the four-letter words.

It would be easier for me to list the horror movies without swears than it would be to rattle off every horror flick with some nasty-ass language. So here it is! The complete list of horror movies without swears in it:

-

And there you have it.

So with all those F-bombs being dropped, it's easy to pick out who's going to get killed—the one who sounds like a trucker. True, murderers may not have the highest moral code—but they seem to dislike potty mouths as much as your Aunt Gert does. So if avoiding the wrath of a killer is at the top of your to-do list, try to keep your language clean.

 SCREAM QUEEN SAYS *Getting your mouth washed out with soap is only the beginning.*

THE MOST F***ED FILM EVER

Spike Lee's *Summer of Sam* tells the true-ish story of an Italian-American Bronx neighborhood terrorized by the Son of Sam killer who went on a killing spree in the summer of 1977. The story is horrifying, especially because the Son of Sam was a very real man (actual name: David Berkowitz) whose crimes terrorized New York City for more than a year.

Also terrifying? The fucking mouths on these people. In fact, *Summer of Sam* clocks in as the most swear-rific horror movie ever with 400 versions of the F-bomb alone. Didn't Spike's mom ever teach him to *Do the Right Thing*?

| SURVIVAL TIP |

KEEP YOUR PLAYLIST LIGHT

YOU EVER HEAR OF ANYONE GETTING CUT WHEN THEY'RE CUTTIN' FOOTLOOSE?

Any good Scream Queen knows you can get freaked out watching a horror movie without ever opening your eyes.

Aside from the screaming and the *chop chop chop, splat* sounds of people getting axed, horror movies are nothing without a killer soundtrack.

From the screeching violins of *Psycho* to the chilling piano notes of the *Halloween* series, the music of horror movies is as well known as their most brutal killing scenes. It's the chicken-and-the-egg scenario of slasher flicks—would the killer still attack if it weren't for that freaky-ass music? Would the smooth sounds of Boyz II Men melt the murderer's heart and keep his bad intentions at bay?

Music has the power to change your mood. Consider how some of our favorite horror movies might have played out differently if the soundtrack had been a little bit lighter:

- Would Michael Myers still have attacked if he had spent his years at the mental institution listening to a carefully crafted mix tape featuring "Peaceful Easy Feeling" by The Eagles, "Night Moves" by Bob Seger, and "The Gambler" by Kenny Rogers?
- Might Carrie's prom have been saved if her senior class song had been "Stairway to Heaven"? The song is so long, they wouldn't have had time to crown Carrie queen, the pig blood disaster would have been avoided, and the night would have ended with corsages being tossed aside and virginity being given up right and left—just the way the good Lord intended proms to end.
- Would Jack still have gone crazy if he'd had a 64 GB iPod? That baby holds 15,000 songs! There is no way things would have gotten dull—even if the weather sucked.
- What if instead of "You Make Me Feel So Dead" and "Fuck This Shit," *Saw* featured songs like Aretha's version of "(You Make Me Feel Like) A Natural Woman"? Perhaps the movie would have been much more *Big Chill* and much

less *Lock People in a Warehouse and Torture Them Until They Saw Their Own Limbs Off.*

 **SCREAM QUEEN SAYS** *Everybody Wang Chung Tonight!*

IF YOU'RE STACKED, CONSIDER A BREAST REDUCTION

HAD I KNOWN I WOULD BE DOING SO MUCH RUNNING, I WOULD HAVE WORN A BETTER BRA.

The hot best friend. The bullying cheerleader captain. The sexy but relatable teacher who knows what it's like to be a teenager these days. What do these cliché movie characters have in common? They're beautiful. They have big boobs. And by the end of the movie, they'll be dead dead dead.

If you happen to be a pretty girl, lucky you. If you happen to be large-breasted, luckier you—unless you happen to be in a horror movie, which means you won't make it to the end of the ninety minutes. See, as long as there have been horror movies, there have been gratuitous shots of girls with huge tater tots running and screaming—and bouncing. It makes for good eye candy. But in real life, there's nothing good about it (aside from the sexy way girls with big chests can fill sweaters in a way their smaller-boobed counterparts cannot).

If we can learn anything from the pervs who direct scary movies, we might as well. We certainly wouldn't want these E-list actresses to be objectified for nothing. So listen, my mammary-blessed friends: before you're forced into a game of survival with a psychopath holding a butcher knife, you may want to consider getting those things reduced.

Who knows why serial killers always target the girl with the D-cups first? Or why our Scream Queen Survivors (think Neve Campbell and Jamie Lee Curtis) are always so, ahem, more proportionate? Perhaps the killers had their hearts broken by big-breasted girls in the past. Or maybe it's because psychopaths enjoy watching girls with big boobies run as much as the next guy? But really, it doesn't matter. The only thing you have to consider is this: if you become the target of a freak with a boob fetish and a murderous vengeance, will it really be worth looking good in a fitted tank top? Perhaps it's time to get those girls tamed.

 SCREAM QUEEN SAYS *How are you supposed to run with those things, anyway?*

DRESS MODESTLY

I'LL JUST THROW ON MY TEDDY AND INVESTIGATE THAT NOISE ON THE FRONT LAWN!

You've already learned about the tendency of killers to target women who are blessed in the chest region. Perhaps this next survival tip is related: if you suspect you are the target of a potential serial killer, it's best to keep yourself buttoned up and tucked in, lest you become the next victim.

This horror movie method of survival defies reason. After all, in most movies, the bad guy with the machete is just that—a guy. However, these dudes, for the most part, had less-than-picturesque childhoods and sway towards the mommy-issue side of the couch (think Norman Bates and Freddy

Kruger). Perhaps that's one reason why the chick with the low-cut shirt, slutty nightgown, or lack of any clothing (save for knee-high gym socks and a ribbon in her ironic braids) always ends up dead.

This is yet another inconvenient survival tip. After all, it's not the clueless girl's fault that horror movies are historically built around sexist ideals or that many take place in the heat of summer. But when you look back on the girls in revealing clothes who were wiped out by serial killers with a seeming dislike for tanned shoulders and running shorts, it's undeniable: if you want to live through a horror movie (or a situation that unfortunately resembles a horror movie), you need to cover up. So, grab that turtleneck, throw on those loose-fitting cargo pants, and stand back while the girls in the Apple Bottom jeans and Juicy tank tops are unfortunately separated from that skin they're so proud of.

Need another reason—or more—to keep that top button fastened? Consider this:

The Top 5 Reasons Not to Dress Like a Slut in Horror Movies, Aside from the Aforementioned Avoiding Death

1. The chance of a boob popping out when you're running from a nut with an axe is exponentially decreased.
2. In any given summer, you'll save dozens of dollars on sunscreen.
3. You'll gain the respect of the guy you're trying to date (who will end up getting picked off after he bangs someone who gives it up within the first twenty minutes of the movie).
4. The chance that the Hot Topic crowd will immortalize your outfit is significantly smaller.
5. Did I mention that not-getting-killed thing?

SCREAM QUEEN SAYS *Your mom was right, less is more.*

GO FOR THE ROMANTIC COMEDIES

THIS RASH OF MURDERS REALLY HAS ME DOWN. I KNOW WHAT WOULD MAKE ME FEEL BETTER—LET'S WATCH *AMERICAN PSYCHO!*

For some reason, the characters in horror movies often turn to the cinematic versions of their own lives to make them feel better. Despite their ability to lighten their current situation, they never opt to watch *Mamma Mia!* One way to guarantee you won't make it out alive: when you think you're in a horror movie or your life is beginning to resemble one, watch a slasher flick.

Hey, life resembles art, right? And this "art" is a bit symbolic for these IQ-challenged, soon-to-be victims. In movie after movie, we see a group of teenagers sit down to watch *The Texas Chainsaw Massacre* or *Halloween III*, seemingly oblivious to the rash of murders closing in around them. And those movie buffs end up on the fast track to DOA.

The Scream Queen has a few theories about why ruthless killers take such issue with those whose Netflix queues are heavy on the horror genre, including:

- disappointment in America's lack of appreciation for the silent film era
- a strong predilection for movie-watching as God intended it—on a drive-in theater screen

- an affinity for America's sweethearts Sandra Bullock and Jennifer Aniston, who rarely show up in horror films (although Jen did star in 1993's *Leprechaun*)
- a dislike for the remakes of horror films, a trend that began in the early 1990s and continues well into the second decade of the 2000s
- deep-rooted feelings of inferiority to the glitzier, more-accomplished killers of the silver screen

Although you're undoubtedly a fan of horror movies (or else, you accidentally picked up this book thinking it was a history of female matriarchs with a tendency to speak at an elevated volume), this survival tip may be a tough one to swallow. But think of it this way: isn't giving up slasher flicks a decent tradeoff for not ending up looking like one of the victims on VHS?

 SCREAM QUEEN SAYS *Stick to* Julie and Julia.

TRUST ME, HE'S NOT DEAD— SO KEEP RUNNING

FINALLY, HE'S DEAD. LET ME JUST CHECK TO MAKE SURE . . .

We've seen this mistake played out on screen dozens of times. In the final standoff between the Scream Queen and the elusive killer, the lone survivor gets her hands on a weapon—a gun, baseball bat, steak knife—and finally takes a whack at the creep who has been picking off her classmates, friends, and family. *Finally, this is it! He's dead*, we think. But, as the camera pans back to reveal the Scream Queen tending to her nearly dead family member who's lying nearby, we see the "dead" killer twitch. He's not done yet.

This mistake is not limited to horror movies such as *The Hitcher* and *Halloween*—we've seen it happen in thrillers including *Fatal Attraction, Sleeping with the Enemy*—hell, we witnessed a tamer version with a happier ending of the "Dead or Alive?" game in *Snow White*. But, when it comes to horror movies, one thing is for sure—the first shot never takes care of him.

The rules of taking down bad guys vary. If you're dealing with a zombie, you'll most likely have to remove a head to decommission him for good. Demons? They're tricky—and usually their Achilles' heel is specific to their method of inhabiting someone else's body. And vampires, well, we always thought the ol' stake through the chest was the only way to waste them but *True Blood* and *Twilight* have taught us alternative methods. And then there are just regular old psychos, who, despite any set rules about how to pick them off, seem to be incredibly resilient.

So if you find yourself proudly standing over the body of a killer you just "effectively" took down, do yourself a favor and put another bullet right through the middle of his forehead. Or, if you're dealing with the undead, tap your knowledge of ways to kill monsters (think silver bullets and wooden stakes) and select the appropriate method to ensure he's a real goner. Because while cinematic history has shown us that eventually the Scream Queen will wipe out her predator, we could do without the heart-pounding, flesh-impaling few minutes of battle that tend to ensue after the killer's initial "death."

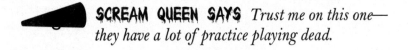 **SCREAM QUEEN SAYS** *Trust me on this one—they have a lot of practice playing dead.*

AN AMERICAN SLASHER WITH JAPANESE ROOTS

In 2002's *The Ring*, two teenagers laugh off a cursed videotape that one of them viewed with a group of friends—which results in the entire group being killed by the undead little girl whose death has haunted the video.

The Ring was a box office hit in the States, spurring a less-than-stellar sequel. But few people know that *The Ring* is actually a remake of a 1998 Japanese film, *Ringu*. If you can put up with the subtitles, consider checking it out. It's scarier than the more widely known American version.

No matter the language, a dead kid climbing out of a television set and running on all fours is enough to keep me from watching a video I know is haunted.

SURVIVAL TIP

QUESTION YOUR INSTINCTS
I ALWAYS KNEW IT WAS YOU!

Pop quiz, Scream Queen fans!

What do the following three characters have in common: a creepy janitor; a quiet kid who keeps to himself; and the old lady who lives alone on the edge of the town who acts, looks, and talks like a witch?

Give up? I'll give you a hint. These people are *never* the killer.

Just as you can safely assume the hottest guy in the bar is always the most disappointing in the sack, you can also trust in this universal truth: the creepiest, likeliest suspect is never actually the one with blood on his hands.

For decades moviemakers have been challenging our assumptions when it comes to whodunit. Perhaps horror flicks have gone the way of our political campaigns and are funded by special interest groups. Think about it. Couldn't People for the Equal Treatment of Scary Old Ladies with a Dozen Cats benefit from an image makeover? Maybe the National Association for Citizens with Hooks for Hands wanted to challenge our stereotypes, and got the ear of a horror movie director. Those hooks can be quite convincing—perhaps they influenced the director to reveal the pretty sorority sister as the killer, instead of the poor, digit-challenged guy who longs for a world where he can run errands without women covering their children's eyes when he walks by.

Keep your wits about you. If you find yourself next up in the line of an unknown killer's likely prey, keep an eye on the handsome jock who lives next door—and be nicer than necessary to the guy with the speech impediment and a limp whose lawn is covered in gremlin statues.

 SCREAM QUEEN SAYS *The guy wearing the "Definitely the Killer" sign is definitely* not *the killer.*

CHAPTER 2

KEEPING YOUR HEAD

It's rare that anyone starts their day contemplating the possibility they'll be hunted and potentially killed before the day is over. But hey, it happens. And when it does, it's almost impossible to not let the fact that your beheading is at the top of someone's To-do List throw you a bit off your game.

In an effort to keep a level-head (hell, or any head at all) while being chased by a guy with knives for hands, this next chapter will give you the ins and outs of staying cool while being murderously pursued.

IF YOU GET AN OFFER YOU CAN'T REFUSE, REFUSE

SURE, I'M HAPPY TO TAKE THIS STASH OF DRUGS AND WAD OF CASH OFF YOUR HANDS IF IT WOULD HELP YOU OUT!

You've probably heard the saying that if something seems too good to be true, it probably is. In horror movies, we have a different saying: if something seems too good to be true, you're probably about to get killed. It may not have the same ring to it and I highly doubt you'll ever see it stitched onto a pillow, but this is one saying that will come in very handy should you find yourself in your own personal horror movie.

Horror films are ripe with people who end up on the wrong side of a machete when they take someone up on a too-good-to-be-true offer. In fact, killers seem to target greedy types by dangling the carrot (usually, the hot and naked carrot) in front of their targets and punishing them for taking a bite. In *Dead & Buried*, a campy and bizarre horror flick from 1981, the movie begins with a young male photographer who encounters a beautiful young woman on the beach. As strangers are prone to do, she offers to let the photographer take nude photos of her. Of course, he would be a fool to turn her down—hey, he really loves his craft. Unfortunately, before he can, ahem, make her say "cheese," a group of crazed townspeople arrive and inexplicably attack him and eventually burn him alive. Maybe he should have thought for a second before he took the hot stranger up on her friendly offer.

We see another instance of the too-good-to-be-true syndrome in *Hostel*. Three horny young backpackers in Amsterdam encounter a man who tells them of a hostel in nearby

Slovakia that is full of hot women just dying to sleep with Americans. Hey, there's no way this could go wrong, right? Well, not exactly. We'll get into the specifics of what happens to these guys in Chapter 4, but for now, let's just leave it at this: they should have stayed in Amsterdam and entertained themselves with low-grade hash.

It's often the dudes in horror flicks who fall victim to the lure of sex, drugs, or money and end up with their gennies cut off. So right there, we Scream Queens have an advantage. However, females have certainly fallen for plenty of handsome guys who end up taking advantage of them (*Carrie* comes to mind) so the only thing you can do here is to stay skeptical. Hey, you wouldn't give out your social security number, date of birth, and cup size to a sketchy stranger who calls to warn you that your credit report is showing suspicious activity. So why would you take fewer precautions when it comes to saving your neck? If you've watched enough horror movies, you're probably well armed with cynicism and skepticism. Why not use it to save your own ass if you find yourself being tempted by fate in the form of a potential killer?

 SCREAM QUEEN SAYS *Looks like that Netflix account may end up paying for itself.*

HORROR WHERE YOU LEAST EXPECT IT: *WILLY WONKA AND THE* CHOCOLATE FACTORY

We all get the chills watching horror movies. But what about those non-horror movies that creep you out beyond belief, when you least expect it?

One such scene is the boat ride in *Willy Wonka and the Chocolate Factory*. Willy, played by the *I'm creepy even when I don't try to be* Gene Wilder, and his guests happily board the *SS Wonka* for a leisurely ride down the chocolate river—only to have Willy go into a (sugar-induced?) trance and appear to lose control of the boat.

Paired with images of a chicken being beheaded, a snake slithering across a corpse, and Willy chanting, "Are the fires of Hell a-glowing/Is the grisly reaper mowing," this scene would have been well received in an axe flick.

Gene Wilder is one weird motherfucker.

LEARN FROM THE MISTAKES OF THOSE WHO CAME (AND WERE KILLED) BEFORE YOU

THIS IS ONE TIME WHEN YOU DEFINITELY DON'T WANT TO KEEP UP WITH THE JONESES.

The word on the street is that the group of kids who disappeared last week—only to be found mutilated—were offed by a vengeful murder victim after watching a haunted DVD/ spending the night in a haunted house/investigating the mystery of the long-abandoned mental hospital on the outskirts of town. What's your next move?

If you answered:

1. Watch the same haunted DVD
2. Spend the night in the same haunted house

3. Investigate the mystery of the long-abandoned mental hospital on the outskirts of town

then I have a final answer for you: You'll get what you deserve.

True, the allure of an unsolved murder may seem slightly sexy, but that's only until your best friend finds you hacked to bits in the linen closet. Yet in movie after movie, we see a determined police officer, loner, or group of teens investigate a murder, only to end up falling victim to the same killer. One word: Duh.

Instead of playing detective, if there's a murder in your neck of the woods, get a clue and get out of town. True, you won't be honored in the local newspaper or given a badge of honor for uncovering the creep behind the crime of the century, but you'll make it out alive. Bonus!

 **SCREAM QUEEN SAYS** *Leave well enough alive.*

| SURVIVAL TIP |

LET SLEEPING DOGS LIE

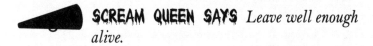

TWO HUNDRED YEARS AGO TONIGHT, A FAMILY WAS HACKED INTO BITS—RIGHT IN THIS VERY HOUSE!

You've no doubt rolled your eyes at this one before. In movie after movie, we've seen this dumber-than-rocks act with a "no shit" ending: doubting the authenticity of a really f'ing creepy legend, a group of determined teens vows to prove once and for all that the lore they've been hearing their entire lives is false. The only problem? That legend is true. So if you live in a town with its own creepy fable, listen up.

Resist the urge to play detective. Steer clear of the library basement, town hall, historical society, or nursing home with loony old residents who were alive for the Creepy Historical Event that your town is known for. Really, stay away from any place that will have you sitting in the dark, skimming old newspapers on microfiche—no good can come from this. Think of it this way: will you feel better if you discover that your strange but harmless elderly neighbor with the familiar face turns out to be the only survivor of a house fire, and he is determined to pay back the descendant of the man who accidentally set the fire (hint: that descendant is *you*)? No, instead you'll let your mom convince you that you're acting weird, and then wake up to said neighbor dousing you with gasoline. But won't you be glad that you learned how to use the library's microfiche machine?

In *The Grudge*, we watched Karen (played by Sarah Michelle Gellar) research the history behind a strange house—and saw her haunted by a little boy who makes bizarre, feline noises and almost get killed about a million times. This horror movie is just one of the many where curiosity almost killed the cat.

This next lesson is a no-brainer. On the anniversary commemorating a horrible event in your town's history, don't throw a freaking party to mock the tragedy. Sure, it might *sound* cute to dress up as the "witches" burned in Salem all those years ago—but the reality is that one of those angry broads is going to come back from the dead to burn you at the stake. Let's see how cute that ends.

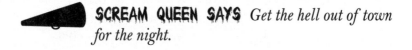 **SCREAM QUEEN SAYS** *Get the hell out of town for the night.*

HOUSE OF BAD ACTING

When audiences previewed House of Wax in 2005, film-makers got a surprise. When Paige (played by the already ubiquitous, sex-tape starring Paris Hilton) was killed via impalement with a metal pole, audiences stood up, cheered, and laughed. Surprising? No. But not exactly the reaction you're looking for when you're previewing a movie designed to actually scare people.

The night-vision shot of Paris giving Shannen Doherty's boyfriend a BJ was way scarier.

DON'T MOCK THE MURDERER
COME OUT, COME OUT, WHEREVER YOU ARE!

It happens in almost every horror movie: a rash of murders torments a small town, college campus, or a city in a country other than the United States. Sick of watching their friends being picked off, a chick playing a tough girl or a scared but fed-up tough guy decides she or he has had enough with waiting around trying to avoid death while their friends disappear like piss-warm Bud Lights at a frat party. Their fate be damned, they turn to mocking the murderer in order to provoke him to action.

They don't care if they're next! They just need to know what's happening! They want to know how the killer has chosen his victims! Mocking the killer, typically on the local news or in a loud voice! Outdoors! With hands thrown to the sky in a frustrated gesture that suggests, "I give up!", the pursued finally decides that he or she is not scared and says something that really pisses off the killer (e.g., "I'm not scared of you," "If it's me you want, come and get me!"). For a second, they almost have us convinced that this will end well. Then, in the very next scene, they eat it—and they eat it bad. To a serial killer, such dismissal is the equivalent of sticking out your tongue while making the "L for loser" sign on your forehead.

Here's a quick lesson about the murdering types: they don't like when someone says to them "fuck you."

So, although you may find a psycho's actions ridiculous and even annoying at times, try to remember a few basics:

- Don't say "fuck you" to the murderer. We can't stress this enough.
- The murderer can always hear you. Always. Even when you think you're just venting to your friends about how not scared you are, someone else can hear you. And that someone else has a meat cleaver.
- Patience will get you far. If you think you've had enough of waiting around, consider the bloody alternative. So don't rush to be the next victim. In horror movies, everyone gets their turn! Try doing something proactive (like hauling ass far away from where the murders are happening) instead of inciting your own demise.

Whatever approach you decide upon, remember this about serial killers: they take their jobs very seriously and don't see the humor in jokes made at their expense.

 **SCREAM QUEEN SAYS** *In that way, they're a lot like mall security guards.*

WHEN IT COMES TO GREAT ONE-LINERS, CONSIDER TRYING FOR SECOND BEST

LET'S SEE A CATTY COMEBACK GET YOU OUT OF THIS ONE.

In most groups of friends (particularly the groups of high school students that populate so many horror movies), there's at least one hot chick with a big mouth—a snappy comeback, a well-timed putdown, or a perfect, under the radar, *you gotta be kidding me* eye roll that can make her friends laugh. But there is a drawback to being the loudest and most sarcastic— as in you might get squashed by the automatic garage door. Not getting me? MALE OR FEMALE, THE LOUDEST MOUTH IN THE GROUP ALWAYS DIES.

Not convinced? Say RIP to smart asses such as Claire (*Prom Night*), Delilah (*The Faculty*), Sasha (*Urban Legends*), and half the sarcastic-as-anything cast of *Scream*. Any way you cut it, killers dislike quick-witted, sarcastic broads as much as the rest of the world does.

Having trouble keeping your cutting tongue in check, despite the threat of having it cut right out of your mouth? Try to focus that verbal energy on better causes. If there's a killer on the loose and you're having a hard time staying quiet, consider keeping your mouth busy in useful ways such as:

- praying that the killer, whose sole mission is to decimate your entire town, decides he's had enough and moves on—before he kills you
- thanking your lucky stars that you're not a slut (Chapter 1), a blonde (Chapter 1), or an undead kid on a tricycle (Chapter 6)

- complimenting the guy who wants to dismember you with a machete, rather than shooting wisecracks at him

Dodging a serial axer is no fun and nothing lightens the mood like some bitchy banter. But when your life is on the line, consider letting the friend who has always lived in your shadow have a bit more time in the spotlight. Just don't be surprised when she turns up dead.

 SCREAM QUEEN SAYS *Hold your tongue if you want it to stay in your mouth.*

SURVIVAL TIP
DON'T IGNORE YOUR VISIONS
THAT VIVID DREAM ABOUT BEING PUSHED DOWN THE STAIRS PROBABLY DIDN'T MEAN ANYTHING ... EVEN THOUGH I WOKE UP TEETERING ON THE TOP STEP.

In movie after movie, we see characters wake up in pools of sweat, shocked by the disturbing dreams they just had. They have visions of horrible accidents, houses being engulfed in flames, tidal waves of blood rushing down hallways, and general chaos, violence, and disaster. On top of these horrors, there is often an in-your-face sign that this nightmare is more than just a dream or vision. You know, the drop of blood inexplicably trickling down the mirror, the smell of smoke when there hasn't been a real fire, the appearance of an ominous word in the fogged-up mirror. Then—surprise, surprise!—the terrifying vision comes to life within the next half-hour.

Learn from the mistakes of all those picked-off chicks who ignored their dreams or violent visions and take those disturbing premonitions seriously. Here are a few signs that your dreams may be omens of things to come:

- Details. In normal dreams, you don't recall what color your fingernails were painted or what song was playing on the car radio next to you while you were sitting at a traffic light. In something-wicked-this-way-comes dreams, however, you do—so remember that and don't speed into the path of an oncoming bus.
- Dream hangovers. If, in your dream, you find yourself running away from a psycho killer and you wake up with sore calves, take that as a warning sign—you weren't just dreaming; you were having a premonition. So stretch your calves and be ready for that stand off, er, run off.
- Leftover items from your dream. A match on your pillow after you dreamt about people perishing in a fire? Dirt in your jacket pocket after you dreamt of being buried alive? Arm yourself with a fire extinguisher and stay on solid ground—your dreams are trying to tell you something.

 **SCREAM QUEEN SAYS** *Sweet dreams are not made of these.*

SURVIVAL TIP

DON'T BOTHER WITH THE FUSE BOX
I'M SURE IT'S JUST THE FUSE BOX. I'LL BE RIGHT BACK . . .

The serial killer is the bane of the house party. Just when people start loosening up and getting drunk (Oops! That's a no-no), getting busy (Damn, that one will end up screwing you, too), and letting the f-bombs fly (Fuck! You're not even supposed to swear!), he has to swoop in and pee on everyone's picnic.

The formula is the same, whether it's *Scream* or *The Slumber Party Massacre*. The first thing the murderer does is fire a warning shot, in the form of leaving a body somewhere for an unsuspecting party guest to find. Before the poor girl (let's face it, it's usually a chick) has a chance to go tell her friends a killer is on the loose, blip! The lights go out. And the entire party is in the dark, unaware of what has happened—and what's coming next.

In most movies, the good hostess goes to check the fuse box—and it's all downhill from there. She finds nothing wrong with the box, then promptly discovers the bodies that have piled up—only to become the next one herself. Then, the partygoers are wiped out, one by one, until only the Scream Queen remains. So how can you avoid all that messy middle stuff before the not-so-happy ending?

Leave the fuse box be. Do not pass go. Do not collect $247 (to reflect inflation). The ol' "let's see her check the fuse box" is equivalent to the teenage boy's yawn-and-boob-grab combination—a classic that you'd be a fool to fall for. So take the Scream Queen's advice on this one. If the fuse box fails, get the hell out of Dodge (whatever that means).

 SCREAM QUEEN SAYS *Do you even know how to check the fuse box?*

SHAUN OF THE DUH

2004's *Shaun of the Dead* is just one of the more recent films that features a character going to check the fuse box. But in this movie, the cliché is turned slightly on its head. First, because the title character, Shaun,

a man, goes to check the fuse box—most often it is
a woman who investigates the lack of lights. Second, Shaun survives the fuse box moment—this is the
moment he realizes the zombies have followed him—and
luckily, is still standing at the end of this ridiculous
horror/comedy.

QUESTION WHY THE WINDOW IS OPEN— THEN LEAVE IT THAT WAY

I DON'T REMEMBER OPENING THAT WINDOW—
I MUST HAVE THOUGH. STRANGE, BECAUSE IT'S JANUARY.
OH WELL!

Murderers are a rude bunch. In addition to the whole ending-
other-people's-lives thing, killers are messy, lack the ability
to make small talk, and rarely knock on the front door when
they enter people's homes. One of their favorite methods of
entrance is through a window. However, they rarely have the
good manners or consideration for your heating bill to close
the window behind them. Cue the clueless chick (or caring,
attentive boyfriend, as in *Prom Night*) who notices the curtain
moving in the breeze—only to shrug off why it's open, chalk-
ing it up to forgetfulness. Strike one. So she closes it. Strike
two. Strike three usually happens when a killer takes a bat to
the girl's head.

The first mistake is not questioning why the window is
even open. Surely, she would have remembered opening it
herself. And of course, because the girl is always home alone
in horror movies, no one could have opened it but her. The
bigger mistake, though, is closing the window. If a psycho has
broken into your house, odds are, you're going to end up in a

chase. And, as in all chases that occur in someone's home, the soon-to-be victim will be trapped without a way to get out. Seems like a good time to have, oh, I don't know, an open window around?

Listen, murderers rarely do anything to help anyone out. Generally speaking, they're "lookin' out for number one" kind of people. So make good use of the one thoughtful thing they do—and leave that window open. Because sooner rather than later, you're going to need to hurl yourself out of it.

 SCREAM QUEEN SAYS *Save yourself some trouble up front—if you see an inexplicably open window, go ahead and jump out of it.*

SURVIVAL TIP

DON'T ASK "WHO'S THERE?" JUST RUN.

WHO'S THERE? [INSERT NAME OF CUTE BOYFRIEND WHOM YOU DON'T REALIZE HAS ALREADY BEEN KILLED], IS THAT YOU?

No one is claiming that the victims in the theater of terror are brain surgeons—we are talking about the girls and guys who make a habit of investigating strange noises, alone, in the dark when a serial murderer is on the loose. But this survival tip seems especially obvious, even to those who have never seen a slasher flick (do such people even exist?): Don't bother catching the name of the guy who's about to behead you. Just run.

Most cold-blooded killers have more to lose than a few kids playing a game of hardcore hide-and-seek. Why then do these ditzes on DVD expect a murderer to go all, "Olly olly oxen free" when they yell out the ubiquitous but ineffective "Who's there?" Have they ever seen a movie where the killer has replied, "I'm the deranged mother of your childhood friend whose accidental death I still blame on you"? Or, "I'm the escaped mental patient with a vengeance for your family due to a long-harbored sense of entitlement over the house you grew up in"? And certainly not, "I'm the new girl from your bio class whose boyfriend was killed in a stunt that your sorority staged years ago but thanks to a genetic glitch, hasn't aged in over twenty years." No, no, and huh?—no.

In the horror genre, a lot of time is wasted on lame and half-assed attempts to escape. Yet asking the shady guy with the meat cleaver to name himself might be the biggest waste of all. Should you find yourself investigating a strange noise (be it a squeaky floorboard, an unexplained *thump!*, or the sound of your long-dead mother's voice crying out for you), and should you have the sneaking suspicion that someone is watching and waiting for you, skip the polite introductions and get the hell out of there.

 SCREAM QUEEN SAYS *If you go this route, you'll be the one who's not there—or anywhere else, for that matter.*

PART 2

WELCOME TO THE JUNGLE

"SAY GOODBYE TO ALL OF THIS . . . AND HELLO TO OBLIVION."
—*THE ROCKY HORROR PICTURE SHOW*

CHAPTER 3

THE GRISLY OUTDOORS

Ah, nature. The stars overhead, the open sky, the smell of sweet, fresh air—the sound of blood-curdling screams? If you've ever seen a horror movie set outdoors (and deny it all you want, but EVERYONE saw *The Blair Witch Project* when it first came out), you know just how freakin' scary the outdoors can be—especially at night. Some of the best slasher flicks ever have pivotal outdoor scenes (hello, *Se7en*). So grab your hiking pack, your cute but outdoorsy hat, and get ready to explore the great, wide, and grisly outdoors.

HEED THE WARNING SIGNS OF WILD ANIMALS

ALL THOSE ANIMALS SEEM TO BE IN AN AWFUL HURRY— LET'S GO SEE WHAT THEY'RE RUNNING FROM!

We've all heard that animals have a sixth sense. Before a natural disaster, animals can be seen running for cover, while humans are still completely unaware of the pending danger. And in horror movies, animals often display warning signs when some serious shit is about to go down. The film characters, however, rarely pay enough attention to these warnings. Unfortunately, ignoring these signs is never a good idea.

In 2009's *Antichrist*, 1984's *Children of the Corn*, and 2009's *Jennifer's Body*—three very different movies—wild animals try to deliver one message: Watch out. Something that freaks out creatures who poop outside is about to go down. And if you don't want to get yourself killed, you'd better run like hell.

Quite frustratingly, the signs from these animals come too late. After noting the strange behavior of the surrounding wildlife in these movies, we see a kid get devoured by the girl he thought he was about to have sex with, a man be brutally tortured by his own wife, and another guy taken down by a group of demon-worshipping teenagers. Even Doctor Dolittle would have been caught by surprise.

Let this be a lesson to you: pay attention to any weird behavior your pets or nearby wildlife exhibit and don't wait until it's too late to seek cover. If your dog starts making guttural noises and tries to hide under your kitchen table, he may just need to throw up the table scraps you unwisely snuck to him. But there's always the possibility he's responding to an evil spirit that is taking over your town. Head for a safe place—preferably not the remote wilderness. The worst thing that will happen if you're wrong is you'll have to clean up a little dog puke. If you're right, well, congratulations. Look who just narrowly avoided being disemboweled!

 SCREAM QUEEN SAYS *The dog whisperer has nothing on you.*

SURVIVAL TIP

AVOID WIDE OPEN SPACES

WHAT'S IN THE BOX?

A creepy (but not in the horror genre) movie your grandparents probably like, 1959's *North by Northwest*, taught us that wide-open spaces can result in disaster—in this case, Cary Grant was chased by a plane and had nowhere to hide. The scene from *Children of the Corn* in the wide-open field provided a, shall we say, eye-opening look at just how much can go wrong in the middle of a cleared space when kids are left in charge, leaving this Scream Queen without any desire to ever step foot in any kind of pasture, meadow, or clearing.

⚠ Apparently, *Se7en's* Detective David Mills never caught *Children of the Corn* on cable and agreed to meet an admitted serial killer using the Seven Deadly Sins to wreak havoc in the middle of freakin' nowhere with only Morgan Freeman to keep him company. No biggie! Turns out he was only being delivered a present—his wife's pretty blonde head in a box. Return to sender! ⚠

If you find yourself faced with an invitation from a suspected killer asking you to meet in an open area with nary a tree to hide under, consider the following options:

- Don't go.
- Suggest an alternative, family-friendly meeting place. Why not split the 2-for-$20 deal at your neighborhood Chili's?
- Show up with your friends—a lot of them. Dress alike, only with each of you wearing slightly different outfits— one of you is missing your brown shoe, another his binoculars, a few without their walking sticks. Leave it up to the killer to find you. Chances are, he'll have so much fun, he'll forget why he came!

 SCREAM QUEEN SAYS *You're bumming if the killer was a* Where's Waldo? *fan.*

WWBPD? OR, WHAT WOULD BRAD PITT DO?

It's hard to imagine 1995's *Se7en* with anyone but Brad Pitt playing Detective David Mills. After all, he met his soul mate (oops, well, soul mate for the mid-nineties) Gwyneth Paltrow on the set of the movie.

Even in the middle of this dark (like, really fucking dark) thriller, as we covered our eyes to block out the disturbing images of John Doe's (expertly played by Kevin Spacey) victims, we just had to take a peek to confirm what we already knew: *Yup, I would still do Brad—even when he's standing over the body of a man whose body actually exploded from over-ingestion.*

But before young Brad accepted the role, it was offered to a better-known actor, the handsome stud that is Denzel Washington. Washington told *Entertainment Weekly* in January, 2010, "They offered me the Brad Pitt part, but I was like, 'This is so dark and evil.' Then, when I saw the movie, I was like, 'Oh shoot.' " Washington stayed busy throughout 1995, starring in *Crimson Tide* and two crappy movies no one ever saw. Care to upgrade that "shoot" to "shit," Denzel?

Turning down a role like that is the Pitts.

BE DISCRIMINATING WHEN OFFERED A LIFT

THIS MAN DRIVING THE VAN WITH CURTAINS OVER THE WINDOW SEEMS LIKE A NICE GUY.

Let's make this quick, shall we? People who hitchhike are stupid. People who pick up hitchhikers are stupid. And people who hitchhike or pick up hitchhikers in horror movies? Really. F'ing. Stupid.

The formula is as old as movies itself. Well, maybe older because detailed, in-depth research (AKA a quick Wikipedia search) tells us that cars were invented in the 1890s whereas silent, black-and-white movies (snorefest!) splashed onto the silver screen in the 1920s. Either way, the hitchhiker in the horror movie conceit has been used a lot—but never more scarily than in 1986's *The Hitcher* or 1974's *The Texas Chainsaw Massacre*. Coincidentally, both were poorly remade in the 2000s.

In *The Hitcher*, a man named Jim Halsey picks up a hitchhiker, John Ryder (I wish I were kidding) who, early on in their ride, offers small talk like, "Wow, you study law? That sounds interesting. See that car by the side of the road? I mutilated the driver. And I plan on doing the same to you!"

THE GRISLY OUTDOORS   49

Jim manages to literally kick John out of his car, only to end up hunted by John and framed for his multiple murders.

⚠ In the end, Jim manages to kill Ryder, but not before his life is in ruins and he has been psychologically tortured. Fun! ⚠

The Texas Chainsaw Massacre features an often-forgotten hitchhiking scene because the bulk of the movie focuses on a group of young people being held captive by the psychotic owners of a slaughterhouse. But let's not overlook the hitch-hiking lesson here: if you pick up a hitcher, not only do you run the risk of getting yourself killed, you also take a chance that this wheelless person could have just escaped from a run-down slaughterhouse and will cut off his own hand while you watch in horror. Good times!

The lesson here? You gotta be kidding me. I think I've made myself pretty clear . . .

 SCREAM QUEEN SAYS *I'm sure there are quicker ways to die, but I can't think of any off the top of my head.*

SURVIVAL TIP

STICK WITH THE GROUP

I THINK WE SHOULD SPLIT UP . . . THAT WAY, ALL THE BODIES WON'T PILE UP IN ONE PLACE.

When it comes to outdoor slasher flicks, this one is a biggie: don't split up. Not into pairs (this will also lessen the odds of you getting lucky, which as we've already covered is a fast track to Murderville). Not into two smaller groups. And especially not off on your own. This will only make you look cocky, and slashers hate cocky.

But these people are driving me frigging nuts! you're think-ing to yourself. *Between the hysterical chick, the muscle-head ego maniac who thinks he'll save all of us, and the creepy goth guy who doesn't seem surprised by any of this, I might kill myself before the murderer can even find us if I don't get away from them!* Let's break this down, shall we?

Think of every horror movie you've ever seen. Think of the people who took off on their own or split into smaller groups. Did this ever end well? I'll name just a few flicks where the characters split up, just to jog your memory:

- *30 Days of Night*
- *The Blair Witch Project*
- *I Know What You Did Last Summer*
- *The Evil Dead*
- *The Descent*

Want to know what happened to all those brave souls who came up with the bright idea to split away from the group? THEY DIED. Weren't you a Girl Scout? Or a Boy Scout? Or some kind of scout who was taught to stick together? Appar-ently, people in horror movies didn't go on any fieldtrips growing up because I *know* this was a biggie in elementary school.

So if you find yourself being stalked by a murderer or two and you're in a big group? Stay that way. Splitting up just spreads the group thin—and makes you easy prey. Like lions, psychotic axers are always looking for the one that breaks off from the herd. No matter how annoyed you get by the freaked out chicks or "I'll save you!" dicks, stick with the crowd.

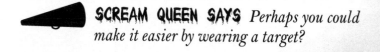 **SCREAM QUEEN SAYS** *Perhaps you could make it easier by wearing a target?*

Remember that PSA about the effects of pollution with the crying Indian, back when we still called people not from India "Indians"? No one likes a litterbug. But desecrating sacred ground—*especially* ground a murderer thinks is sacred—is an even bigger no-no. In this case, you'd be the one who's crying.

We saw this played out (with not-so-great results) in *The Blair Witch Project*. Three almost completely unlikable twenty-something filmmakers set out to investigate the mystery of the Blair Witch who supposedly lived and terrorized deep in the woods of Shitsville, Maryland. While in search of an ancient cemetery, the three discover little straw figures in the shape of people hanging from the trees, as well as oddly but purposely placed piles of rocks. In a less-than-smooth move, one of the filmmakers accidentally kicks the pile of rocks over. And it's lights out from there.

In both the 1978 and 2008 versions of *Long Weekend*, a couple who goes camping for the weekend shows disrespect for Mother Nature. When they're not hell-bent on taking each other down, they seem hell-bent on taking down the environment. They throw lit cigarette butts into the brush and beer bottles into the ocean, and chop down trees just for the hell of it. In the 2008 version, the couple's vacation is more beachy but the premise is the same—the horribly unhappy couple strives to reconnect and destroy the environment at the same time.

⚠ In a twist on typical horror revenges, this time it's the flora and fauna that strike back. Animals begin to attack the couple—possums, impossibly huge spiders, and bald eagles alike stalk their prey until the couple ends up on the endangered species list. Just goes to show you that everybody hates people who don't respect the Great Outdoors. ⚠

Now, I know you wouldn't be so insensitive. But whether hiking in the boonies of Maryland or taking a vacation with your BF, the message here is clear. Don't mess with other people's land. Just because someone is a witch (or a mere force of nature) doesn't mean they're forgiving. So watch where you step, and when on vacation be sure to bring that reusable tote and recycle your beer bottles. Haven't you ever heard of "carry in, carry out"?

 SCREAM QUEEN SAYS *Repeat after me: Reduce, Reuse, Recycle or you might find yourself composted.*

| SURVIVAL TIP |

UPGRADE YOUR CELL SERVICE

I SAID I'M BEING HUNTED BY A PSYCHOPATH . . . CAN YOU HEAR ME NOW? HOLD ON A SECOND, I'LL STEP OUTSIDE.

For years, we watched horror movies and thought to ourselves, *God, if only that girl had a cell phone she never would have been trapped at the bottom of a well/buried alive in a remote area of the desert/forced to choose between sawing her arm off or being blasted to death by a steam pipe.* We stood by helplessly in film after film as a soon-to-be murder victim tries to use a land line to call for help, only to find that the phone wires have been cut.

Finally, in the 2000s (about ten years after everyone had their own), the cell phone began to make its way into slasher films. *This is it!* we thought, breathing a collective sigh of relief. *At least now, these helpless broads can call someone else for help.* Oh, how wrong we were.

Statistically speaking, in horror movies, cell phones work approximately 0.0000000037 percent of the time. Whether it's due to a low battery or crappy service, the usefulness of the cell phone belonging to the character in danger is reduced to that of a digital thermometer. You gotta wonder, what kind of phone does this chick have? Jitterbug? Although we've all had our moments when we stood on top of coffee tables holding our phones high above our heads, desperately trying to pick up a signal strong enough to place an all-important late night take-out order, I doubt that *anyone*, even those anyones living in the middle of nowhere, have had one fraction of the number of problems finding a reliable cell phone network that girls in slasher flicks do.

So at least try to give yourself a fighting chance here. Whether you're fighting off a guy with a hook for a hand or just trying to get a tow service to pick your ass up on a shady stretch of highway, do yourself a favor and upgrade your cell phone—and then keep that baby charged. Because you never know when you're going to have to call 911— for a flat tire or to share the news that the escaped inmate wanted for your attempted murder has been found (in your backseat).

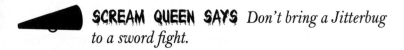 **SCREAM QUEEN SAYS** *Don't bring a Jitterbug to a sword fight.*

NO SIGNAL, NO ESCAPE

Still don't believe me? Here are just some of the horror movies that feature cellular drama: *Killer Movie, Rest Stop, Joy Ride: Dead Ahead, Vacancy, Jeepers Creepers* (the cell is referred to as a "portable phone" in this dinosaur), *Dead End*, *Detour*, *When a Stranger Calls*, *The Mist*, *The Ruins*, *The Hills Have Eyes*, *The Evil Woods*, *Turistas*, *House of the Dead*, *Saw*, *Saw V*, *Last House on the Left*, *The Gingerdead Man*, *The Abandoned*, *House of Wax*, *Hostel*, *Urban Legends: The Final Cut*, *One Missed Call*, *The Hitcher*, *The Strangers*, *30 Days of Night*, *Alien Versus Predator*, *The Signal*, *Quarantine*, and *Open Water 2* (in this one, they expected the phone to work after it had been dropped in—you guessed it!—water. Those idiots deserved what they got.).

Bottom line: You'd be better off using smoke signals.

SURVIVAL TIP

STAY ON YOUR FEET

I'VE NEVER HAD SUCH A HARD TIME STAYING UPRIGHT ... PERHAPS I'M DISTRACTED BY THE PERSON CHASING ME WITH A BUTCHER KNIFE.

The "run from the killer" scene is one of the best parts of the horror film genre. Whether it's a frantic chase through a house with the killer right on the heels of our Scream Queen; a highway chase, with the unrelenting lights in the rearview mirror; or an ambling, slow speed chase over the uneven ground of darkened woods, it's always the part of the movie that makes our pulse race and our hands sweat.

But when we're not yelling at the screen, illogically cheering on the poor girl whose fate has been sealed long before we came into the picture, we're hitting our hands against our foreheads, dumbfounded at this chick's bad luck: the poor thing can't stay on her feet. She's tripping up the stairs, she's stumbling over fallen logs, she's crashing through loose floorboards. And through it all, we're thinking, *how many times can this chick fall?*

Everyone has fallen at inconvenient times or stood by and watched someone else take a digger, embarrassing and sometimes injuring themselves in the process. But there is never a less opportune time to fall than when you're running for your frigging life. And while this is not one of those situations you can prepare for, there are a few ways you can give yourself a better chance of making it out alive should you find yourself being hotly pursued by someone whose sole mission is to take your life.

First of all, consider who's chasing you and adjust your speed accordingly. Spry young mental institution escapee chasing you down the main street of your town? Go balls out immediately, heading toward anyplace where there may be other people to help you, or at least somewhere to hide. Resurrected zombie with half of a leg missing, ambling toward you over hilly farmland, a la *Night of the Living Dead*? Keep it at a brisk jog—those guys are slow, but not as slow as you may think. Battling someone or something in between (creepy little kid coming at you on a tricycle, undead fisherman still recovering from being killed in a car crash)? Keep your pace brisk but watch your step. After all, no matter who—or what—you're running from, it won't matter how fast you are if you end up falling and breaking a leg. Like we've seen on Nat Geo, the weakest of the pack always ends up ripped to pieces.

 **SCREAM QUEEN SAYS** *Never underestimate the importance of sensible shoes.*

STAY OUT OF THE ABANDONED CABIN

ANYBODY IN HERE?

This is one of those survival tips that I can't even believe I have to tell you. To me, the phrase "abandoned cabin" elicits horrifying images of bodies being hidden under loose floorboards, people running screaming into the night where only the wildlife can hear you—and truly skin-crawling factors like peeing in a port-o-potty and reading by flashlight. But for some idiots, e.g. people who like camping and teenagers who would go anywhere to get away from their parents' watchful eyes, the lure of an empty cabin in the woods is too much to resist.

However, it only takes a few horror movies to show just how awry things can go when you take away civilization and all that comes along with it (electricity, access to a hospital, a responsive police unit). If you're still considering a jaunt to a remote cabin in the great outdoors, remember how it ended up for some of our slasher flick friends.

⚠ In *Evil Dead II*, Ash, lone survivor of the first *Evil Dead*, takes his girlfriend Linda to a cabin where, oops!, he accidentally reawakens The Evil Force, which takes over Linda's body, resulting in her quite literally losing her head. Ash is forced to cut off his own hand with a chainsaw, and is ultimately named the unlikely and unwilling king of The Evil Force. Just think how much better his weekend could have been if he had only stayed at home. ⚠

In *The Ring*, a group of teenagers head to a cabin in the woods and accidentally unleash yet another evil spirit, this one of a little girl whose own mother threw her down a well where she toiled for seven days before dying. Through a worn-out VHS tape, these teenagers start a chain of unfortunate murders—all because they wanted to drink cheap beer and have promiscuous sex.

⚠ Speaking of wanton sex and booze, in *Cabin Fever*, a group of recent college grads rent a cabin for a week to partake in a lot of both. After one of them accidentally shoots a weird hermit/transient type, they refuse to help him and instead dump his disease-ridden body in a reservoir . . . which they then drink from via tap water. One by one, they fall victim to a horrible, flesh-eating disease. ⚠

And then there's the king of freaky-ass abandoned cabin movies, *The Blair Witch Project*. Without actually showing a witch, gore, or killing, this movie manages to scare off anyone with half a brain in their head from ever entering an abandoned cabin—thanks largely to a suspenseful scene in which the three obnoxious-as-all-hell twenty-somethings finally find the Blair Witch.

I could go on. But I think by now you see where I'm going with this one: there's a reason why those abandoned cabins are, well, abandoned.

 SCREAM QUEEN SAYS *Check out Travelocity before booking your next vacation.*

SURVIVAL TIP

CHECK YOUR BATTERY, GAS, TIRES, AND FLUIDS

DAD WAS RIGHT. I SHOULD HAVE TAKEN MY CAR IN EVERY 3,000 MILES.

In horror movies, the only thing to malfunction more often than cell phones (see Upgrade Your Cell Service) are cars. Whether it's parked right in front of someone's house or in the middle of the freaking woods, whether it's a brand new Dodge Ram or an old piece of shit, doesn't matter in the slightest—that thing is not starting. Or maybe it will start—only to immediately get a flat tire. Or maybe the car will make an unexplained noise, accompanied by a cloud of smoke when the driver looks under the hood. Here's a survival tip that will aid you in the long run: keep that car of yours tuned up. If you find yourself in the middle of a horror movie, you're going to need it. After all, we know you can't rely on your feet (see Stay Off Your Ass).

There's no logical reason for cars to break down so often in slasher flicks. After all, most horror movies take place long after the time when you had to crank the car to get it started. But logical or not, it's the reality of horror flicks. Still don't see the value in keeping your car fueled, lubed up, and running on regularly rotated tires? Consider just some of the movies where characters were beaten, bludgeoned, and beheaded all because they didn't properly maintain their vehicles (or possibly because a serial killer purposely sabotaged their wheels):

- *Halloween*
- *I Know What You Did Last Summer*
- *Jeepers Creepers*
- *The Texas Chainsaw Massacre*
- *House of Wax*
- *Wolf Creek*
- *P2*
- *When a Stranger Calls*

When it comes to scary movies, there's no guarantee about cars—we've seen brand new whips fail to start in the most inconvenient of situations. But give yourself a fighting chance and take care of your car. After all, your freaking life may depend on it.

SCREAM QUEEN SAYS *People who run out of gas get what's coming to them.*

HOLD THAT SIGH OF RELIEF UNTIL DAYLIGHT

WE'RE FINALLY SAFE! NOW ONLY IF IT WERE LIGHT OUTSIDE. WAIT, WHAT'S THAT NOISE?

Have you ever noticed how things always seem better in the light of day? You get in a fight with your boyfriend at a party and go home red-eyed and devastated—only to wake up feeling receptive to his "Sorry" text message and a bit remorseful yourself. Or you get out of bed in the morning feeling like you could run a marathon, when just the night before you were convinced you'd never lose those last five pounds you've been trying to shed. Well, horror movies are no different.

Anyone in any slasher flick who ever thought she was safe while it was still dark out had quite another thing coming. If night seems endless in horror movies, that's because it is. There's nothing scary about the daytime—in fact, the only daylight we see in most horror movies is in the opening *it was a day like any other* montage when the main character is seen going about his or her business, unaware of the hell that's about to break loose. All the bad stuff starts happening when it's dark out. Thunderstorms, murderers, psychopaths, true identities (identities with a vengeance, that is) revealed—it all goes down after dark. That's why it's so surprising when, in what we know to be the eye of the storm, a character thinks things have actually gone back to normal—while it's still frigging dark out. Fooled by the "killer" being taken down, the people who have been terrorized are relieved, believing that their fight for life is over. But newsflash to these unobservant suckers who have already fallen for the too-obvious-to-be-true identity of the killer: things are never over until the sun comes up.

Whether you're watching a slasher flick or running from someone who wants to slash you into bits, never let your guard down until the night is over. Most rules in horror flicks are meant to be broken. But when it comes to light versus dark, one is unquestionably scarier than the other—and you're unquestionably being a dumbass if you think you're safe before daybreak.

 SCREAM QUEEN SAYS *It doesn't matter if you're talking break-ups or beheadings: everything seems better in the A.M.*

SURVIVAL TIP

FOR GOD'S SAKE, STAY OUT OF THE WOODS

IF THE KILLER DOESN'T GET YOU, THE POISON IVY WILL.

Very rarely do you ever hear about someone going into the woods and having it end well.

Sure, there are people like Henry David Thoreau who walk into the woods and come out unscathed—with no horror stories of unexpected rainstorms and leaky tents or insane hikers and ritualistic dismemberment. But those people are few and far between. You only hear about the ones who go into the woods, only to return physically or mentally scarred—or don't return at all.

In my mind, this isn't a tough tip to swallow. I'm not telling you to give up Caribbean vacations or bikini waxes—we're talking about the friggin' woods. So, repeat after me: no hiking, no camping, no backpacks, no trails, no campfires, no sleeping outside with only a thin layer of canvas between you and the elements, which include inclement weather, wild animals, and psychotic types who enjoy hacking cute girls in sleeping bags into bits.

From *Just Before Dawn* to *The Blair Witch Project* to *Sleep Away Camp,* the formula for survival in the outdoors, specifically the woods, has been made pretty clear: don't go there. That Thoreau guy may have deliberately decided to live in the woods but if you want to deliberately avoid death, I'd suggest keeping that hiking backpack in the closet and that butt of yours on the couch.

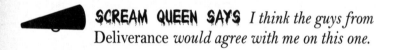 **SCREAM QUEEN SAYS** *I think the guys from* Deliverance *would agree with me on this one.*

SURVIVAL TIP

DON'T FORGET YOUR GPS

I'M SURE THIS NICE MAN CAN TELL US HOW TO GET BACK TO THE HIGHWAY!

Killers are lazy. They're not looking to exert any more energy than necessary. Don't believe me? Have you ever seen these lazy bastards run? You're lucky if you even see them break into a brisk walk.

When it comes to getting things done, killers often take the easy way out. They probably use Peapod to do their grocery shopping and have signed up for automated bill paying. So, when they're in the mood to slash some throats, you can bet they're going to seek out easy targets. And there's no target easier or more vulnerable than someone who doesn't know where the hell she's going.

Horror movies often depend on the formula of people getting lost, picked off, and found when only one or none is left. However, a couple movies stand out from the rest.

The first is one that everyone has seen: *The Blair Witch Project*. Too distracted by their own agenda and inability to get along with each other, the filmmakers end up miserably lost while seeking out the truth behind a string of murders some decades earlier. Although they didn't have the luxury of GPS (nerds hadn't gotten around to inventing one yet), they did have a map that they failed to read correctly and then (big mistake) got rid of out of frustration about being lost. ⚠ No surprise ending here: they never made it out of the woods. ⚠

In a lesser-known British movie, 1970's *And Soon the Darkness*, two girls on a cycling vacation take a break at a bar in a rural area and choose to pursue some local tail rather than plan their route. Once they're back on the road, they find themselves lost. And in case breaking one survival rule wasn't enough, they argue and split up. ⚠ In the grand tradition of horror movies, each encounters some twisted locals and things go downhill from there. ⚠

While GPSs were not available to the *Blair Witch* kids or the doomed cyclists, each group failed to make proper use of the technology they had—their maps. And hey, if you don't make use of the resources available to you, then you won't garner too much sympathy from the horror movie crowd.

Things have changed since those movies were made (and when the American version of *And Soon the Darkness* comes out in 2011, you'll hope they'll at least use Google Maps on their phones), and now there's no excuse for ever getting lost. So charge your iPhone, put your route into your GPS before you even leave the driveway, and when the computerized voice tells you to take a right in 800 yards, you best take that right.

 **SCREAM QUEEN SAYS** *It's hard to "recalculate" after you've been beheaded.*

CHAPTER 4

FREAKY LOCALES

Or, as I'd like to call it, the "No Shit" section of the book.

There are lots of places where you'd have to be half-insane to visit. Abandoned mental institutions. Post-apocalyptic cities where virus-infested zombies reign supreme. Trenton, New Jersey. But many horror movies wouldn't exist if it weren't for the stupid, insane, or just plain unlucky people who go into places as scary—and scarier—as the places we'll cover in this section. So grab your flashlight and a jacked-up guy to go ahead of you, and get ready to explore these hauntingly freaky locales.

STAY THE HELL OUT OF MAINE

YOU CAN'T GET THERE FROM HERE . . . OR GET OUT OF HERE ALIVE.

Every year, thousands of families head to Maine for fun in the sun or to hit the slopes. Something about the fresh air and remote wilderness brings out the best in those whose idea of a perfect vacation involves campfires, marshmallows, and spotty cell service. And then there are the college kids who take advantage of their friend-of-a-friend's grandparents who own a lake house they never use. This crowd thinks of Maine as a place to get drunk and screw while enjoying the smell of pine. Between the beers, lakes, and lobsters, it's no wonder Maine state license plates proudly display the phrase, "Vacation Land."

Unfortunately, the people who live in Maine don't enjoy it the same way the vacationers do. Mainers are a stereotypically kind but simple folk; however, the general consensus of the rest of the country is that year-round residents of the Pine Tree State spend their time bitching about the annoying tourists who jam their highways and blow their natural resources to shit—that is, when they're not cursing the fact that their tourist industry is on the decline. Either way, they're still less annoying than the tourists.

In horror movies, though, we see a whole different side of Maine. The killers you find in these horror flicks vary as much as Mark Wahlberg's accent in every movie he's ever been in. You've got your zombie pets, a pissed-off gypsy, a nondescript lake monster, run-of-the-mill psychos hell-bent on revenge, the demon spirit of a woman falsely accused of being a witch—it's a veritable who's who of killers.

Why so many horror movies set in Maine? The Scream Queen has a few theories. It could be due to the remote wilderness and the common belief that remote wilderness tends to drive people a little bit cuckoo. It could also have something to do with the fact that the master of horror, Stephen King, hails from Maine—and many of the movies based on his novels take place there. You'll see a few of them on this list that contains just a handful of the horror flicks set or filmed in What a Shitty Vacation This Turned Out to Be Land:

- *Pet Sematary*
- *Thinner*
- *Prophecy*
- *Darkness Falls*
- *It*
- *Lake Placid*
- *The Mist*

Luckily, Maine is not one of those states you'll find yourself having to drive through often. In fact, no one really has to go to Maine unless it's his final destination—and, if the movies have taught us anything, it may very well be. So when you find yourself hankering for some skiing or lakeside recreation, consider the neighboring state of New Hampshire. Hell, why not go to Canada? Not even a serial killer wants you dead so badly that he would go there.

 **SCREAM QUEEN SAYS** *Vacationland or not, you're better off in Vermont.*

STAY ON THE GROUND FLOOR

I KNOW HOW I'LL GET AWAY FROM THIS PSYCHO— I'LL RUN UPSTAIRS!

I have to chalk up the need for this survival tip to sheer panic. After all, who the hell would head to the top floor of her house to escape a killer? It's not as if brutal sociopaths have an aversion to the common household staircase or a physical inability to climb more than three steps. They also don't become lightheaded when they are in elevations higher than thirteen feet above sea level. If you're a horror movie fan, you know that, unfortunately, this is just wishful thinking. You also know that when you see a chick chased up the stairs, it's not going to end well.

You've heard of the Darwin Awards, right? The prize given posthumously to those who improve our gene pool by removing themselves from it through incredibly stupid, accidentally self-inflicted deaths? Well, I proudly nominate every single movie character who ran upstairs. I ask: what is wrong with the front door? Even if the killer is blocking it, you leave yourself with only two outcomes by trapping yourself upstairs: the killer eventually gets you because you run out of places to hide, or you end up having to jump out the window—only to have him get you once you're lying on the ground outside with both legs broken.

The lesson here? Just don't let yourself get chased upstairs. It's the exaggerated, life-threatening version of mopping the kitchen floor without leaving yourself a path to get out. Only the outcome is typically much more unpleasant than damp socks.

 **SCREAM QUEEN SAYS** *I'm kind of annoyed that I even needed to point this one out.*

CHECK OUT THE BACKSEAT

LET ME JUST ADJUST MY REARVIEW MIRROR AND . . . OH, NO. HIM AGAIN.

Your mother probably told you this one before you went off to college—before you get in your car, check behind the front seat to make sure no one is waiting to attack you. Looks like the girls in horror movies didn't listen to that advice. We've seen far too many people in movies like *Urban Legend* and *Zombieland* hop into their cars without a thought—and never make it to their destinations. Bummer.

The ol' psycho-in-the-backseat trick is not limited to the horror genre. In thrillers, we often see the protagonist slide behind the wheel of her car, only to feel the business end of a gun on the back of her neck and hear a quick order to, "Drive!" More often than not, she ends up living. But in slasher flicks we usually see a different outcome. The poor chick barely has a chance to get her key in the ignition before a murderous dude without a care in the world (or license of his own) puts a knife to her throat—and then it's lights out.

So do yourself a favor and for once, listen to your mother. Check out that backseat. This is one time she's right—and proving her wrong is not worth dying.

 SCREAM QUEEN SAYS *It will be hard to drive when your head is riding shotgun.*

LOOK OUT BEHIND YOU

I CAN'T FIND THIS MURDERER ANYWHERE! HE MUST HAVE LEFT. OH, WELL. BACK TO THE SLEEPOVER!

It's a cinematic cliché that originated in horror flicks but has made its way into every film genre. Even today, time and time again, we find ourselves throwing our hands up in disbelief and yelling, "LOOK OUT BEHIND YOU!"

From Jodie Foster, sporting night vision goggles and fumbling through Buffalo Bill's basement in *The Silence of the Lambs*, to Shelley Duvall in *The Shining*, running around like a chicken with her head cut off, holding a butcher knife in the way a teenage girl handles her first boyfriend's naughty bits, we watch these Scream Queens endure way more than they have to in order to survive—all because they didn't look behind them.

Before you know it, these forward-watching damsels are tossed to the ground, pushed down a flight of stairs, or getting their throats slit from behind. How to avoid an equally disturbing fate? Easy. Try walking backwards! Visit your local museum or college campus, ask for a tour, and be prepared to watch some backwards-walking magic. These knowledgeable folks can tell you the history behind the oldest building on campus, how to distinguish the work of a French postmodernist from a neo-classical Italian, and where you can find the restrooms—all without ever taking a single step forward. Certainly, they can show you a thing or two about watching your back while investigating a strange noise or mysteriously absent party guest.

 **SCREAM QUEEN SAYS** *What are you doing investigating strange noises to begin with?*

WHEN YOUR PARENTS GO AWAY FOR THE WEEKEND, GO WITH THEM

YOU COULD REALLY USE MOM OR DAD'S HELP ON THIS ONE.

The lure of an empty house, a keg of beer, and some horny coeds is enough to make any guy get excited. But when the big news of the summer is a serial murderer on the loose who has been targeting teenage girls and young women, consider trading the freedom of staying home alone for a weekend of family bonding—if only for your own survival.

Even your own bedroom can seem like the creepiest place on earth when you know mom and dad aren't on the other side of your door to help you should you hear a thing go bump in the night or a guy with a chainsaw rip through your front porch. Without their car in the driveway and your dad's unfaltering ability to be ready with a flashlight and his pair of tighty-whities whenever you hear a strange noise, even home sweet home can take on a sinister feel.

Before you start calling me a goody two-shoes, let's take a look at how wrong your night on your own can go versus what family memory you may miss out on:

WHEN YOU GO AWAY WITH YOUR PARENTS, YOU MAY:	WHEN YOU STAY AT HOME ON YOUR OWN, YOU MAY:
Be forced to suffer the indignity of getting a picture taken with a Disney character you're way too old to think is cool	Be forced to suffer the indignity of having a picture taken of your individual limbs as they are severed from your body and sent to the local newspaper
Eat a few too many ice-cream cones, courtesy of Mom and Dad	Eat a combo of Pop Rocks and Draino, courtesy of a jilted psychopath

WHEN YOU GO AWAY WITH YOUR PARENTS, YOU MAY:	WHEN YOU STAY AT HOME ON YOUR OWN, YOU MAY:
Arrive home with a sunburn, due to a few too many hours on the beach	Arrive home with a sunburn, due to being baked in a tanning bed by an undead fisherman who's still pissed at you for running him over with your car
Get caught rolling your eyes the third time your father tells you to "Smile for the birdy!" into the camera	Get caught with your eyes rolling out of your head the third time you say "Candyman" into your mirror

So although neither situation sounds like a good time, it's clear that staying home on your own can lead to a shitty outcome (and that's putting it mildly. Did I mention the severed limbs?). Throw out that idea of beer bongs and coed sleepovers, hop into the minivan, and get ready for some family bonding. Even if you can only manage to grin and bear it, it's better than being strung bare-ass nekkid on the tree in your backyard.

 SCREAM QUEEN SAYS *At least you'll keep all your appendages.*

SURVIVAL TIP

DON'T GO LOOKING FOR YOUR PET IN A DARK AND SKETCHY PLACE

THAT ABANDONED BUILDING WITH SMASHED OUT WINDOWS IS FAR TOO DANGEROUS FOR MY DOG TO EXPLORE . . . I'M GOING TO HEAD IN AND GET HIM.

Devotion to a pet is, for the most part, a very admirable trait. You can learn a lot about a guy you're interested in by watching him with his animal companion. Does he throw his beloved Golden table scraps that more closely resemble a petite filet than any scrap you've ever seen? Does he sleep with his cat curled up on the foot of his bed, or, perhaps a bit creepily, with her right under the covers with him? Yes, some people take devotion to their animals a bit too far, especially in horror movies. Sure, you never want to see anything bad happen to an animal. But sometimes, you have to check your priorities. After all, it's pretty hard to keep your pet safe if you're locked up in some psycho's dungeon.

In 2007's *I Am Legend*, Will Smith plays Robert Neville, the last man on earth. His only companion is his loyal German Shepherd, Samantha. Neville spends his days researching possible cures for the virus that has transformed the entire human population into zombies, and Sam never leaves his side. Unfortunately, they are only free in the daylight, as the sunphobic zombies take over the world at night and hide in dark shadows during the day.

During one of their treks throughout the deserted New York City, Sam runs away from Robert and heads into a pitch-black, abandoned building—one that is likely home to dark-seeking zombies. Like a true idiot, Robert goes right in after her and almost gets them both killed in the process.

It may sound cruel to suggest that you let your beloved pet fend for herself if you find yourself hiding out from murderers (human or not). But why not put her on a leash? Sure, this may look a bit strange if your animal companion is a cat . . . but if your best friend is a cat, it's probably not the first time that you've been accused of being a bit of an oddball.

 **SCREAM QUEEN SAYS** *Crazy Cat Lady sounds like it could be a blockbuster horror movie.*

HIT AND YOU BETTER RUN

I'LL JUST LEAVE THIS GUY I JUST HIT WITH MY CAR TO REST AND RECOVER ... AT THE BOTTOM OF THE HARBOR.

We owe a lot to the box office smash *I Know What You Did Last Summer.* After the 1980s slasher fad died out, the horror genre suffered an identity crisis, going through a bit of a sci-fi hybrid phase and churning out unwatchable crap such as *Arachnophobia*, *Alligator II*, and *Critters*.

Scream (1996) and *I Know What You Did Last Summer* (1997) gave the genre a one–two punch of reinvention that continued well into the early 2000s, before the Remake Era started. And thanks to the latter of the two films, our boyfriends will forever compare how our boobs look in a strappy tank top to Jennifer Love Hewitt's.

⚠ Due to its popularity and somewhat ridiculous but still enjoyable plot line, *I Know What You Did Last Summer* was often parodied—think of the hysterical satire of horror flicks, *Scary Movie*—and not without reason. It would be easier for me to list which survival tips the teenagers featured in this movie *didn't* ignore. They drank, had sex, mocked the murderer, had big jugs they weren't afraid to show off in their skimpy clothes while competing for the loudest and most obnoxious of the group—you name it, these dumbass characters did it. It was almost as though they wanted to be picked off one by one—and so they were, save for our Scream Queen, Julie, the aforementioned busty Jennifer Love. And because they gave me so much material to work with (read: mock), I figured the least I could do was to pay homage to their big frigging bad: running over a dude and leaving him to die—without making sure he was actually a goner. ⚠

If you're reading this book, you've probably seen this movie. And if you haven't, I don't want to ruin the ending for you—somehow, I think I might end up being, ahem, punished for that. But I will give you a down-and-dirty survival guide based on this unlikely classic:

- If you've been drinking, stay off a long stretch of abandoned, creepy highway. Creepy people are bound to be behind every guardrail or walking down the yellow line.
- Don't run over anyone.
- If you do run over someone, makes sure he's dead before you decide the best way to dispose of him is throwing him in the harbor, lest he come back to kill you.

The end.

 SCREAM QUEEN SAYS *No matter how good a movie, that* Ghost Whisperer *chick is one annoying twit.*

SURVIVAL TIP

WHEN STUCK IN A SKETCHY SPOT, DON'T MAKE PLANS FOR TOMORROW

THE FIRST THING I'M GOING TO DO WHEN I GET OUT OF HERE IS . . .

When you're stuck in a creepy and horrible place, it's natural to fantasize about what you're going to do when you get out of there. On a particularly dreary Monday morning, sitting at your desk at work, you've no doubt already found yourself e-mailing your friends to make plans for the weekend. Or six minutes into what you've sworn will be a sixty-minute stint on the elliptical machine, you're already thinking about your drive-through dinner on the way home. And when you're being held captive someplace miserable at the mercy of a serial killer, it's no wonder that you may find yourself thinking about what you'll do when—and if—you ever get out of there.

Here's where optimism fails us, though. Because there's an unfortunate history of horror movie characters stuck in freaky, isolated places (haunted cabins, industrial garages, the underbelly of the New York subway system) who have verbalized their plans for after they get back to the real world. The problem? Those people never see the real world, or anywhere else, ever again.

This is similar to the "I'll be right back" syndrome. No one knows if this is a coincidence or if psychotic killers have an active dislike for unreasonable optimism. Perhaps the Pollyannas are distracted by their daydreams and take their eyes off the 8-ball for a minute, leaving them susceptible to the person whose mission is to waste them. Whatever the reason, you should really be most concerned about the ultimate outcome. If you find yourself at the mercy of a murderous nut, resist the urge to make plans for when you get back to your normal life—if you do indeed get to live. Keep your wits about you, keep your focus on the task at hand, and bite your lip as to that mani-pedi you plan on getting once your hands and feet aren't chained together.

 SCREAM QUEEN SAYS *Even non-murderers agree that the glass-half-full shit can get tiring after a while.*

MY BAD: F-UPS ON FILM: DAYBREAKERS

Dozens of slasher flicks involve mistaken-for-dead characters. Yet, in 2009's *Daybreakers*, you couldn't blame anyone for thinking that Frank, a greedy human-turned-vampire-turned-human, might still be alive even after his blood is drained. When the camera pans over him, despite the fact that he is dead—Frank's eyes flutter. Surprisingly, the actor who played Frank (Michael Dorman) didn't receive any Oscar love for his performance.

SURVIVAL TIP

RECONSIDER THAT ROAD TRIP

FOR SPUR-OF-THE-MOMENT FUN ON THE ROAD, DON'T FORGET TO PACK YOUR SUNSCREEN, CELL PHONE CHARGER, AND STEEL-CUTTING SAW.

When it comes to technology, horror movies are a bit behind the times. Whereas the rest of us seem to have at least marginally functioning cell phones, as we've already covered, those characters walk around with glorified calculators. And it's no different when it comes to travel. Most of us hop on Travelocity or Trip Advisor when we want to go somewhere, but teenagers and twenty-somethings in horror movies are still holding on to the long-lost art of the road trip—and inevitably opt for the dark and scary side road over the well-lit and busy highway.

Whether they're heading to a concert, a camping trip, or a beach week, people in horror movies are driving. Featuring cheesy pop music, montages of the nation's tourist spots, and way more high-fives than necessary, the road trip is a horror movie standby, especially when it comes to teenager slasher flicks. But unfortunately, not only do these teens risk carsickness and speeding tickets, they usually end up at the mercy of a freak who has been waiting for a carload of kids to come by to add to his collection.

Although this Scream Queen is no big fan of flying, or, more specifically crashing, there's just too much that can go wrong on a road trip that involves desolate rest stops, sparsely-populated cut-through towns, and rural bumpkins looking to dine on some kids from the big city. As we've discussed, car problems run rampant in horror movies and, on road trips especially, the car tends to overheat/run out of gas/ get a flat on the creepiest, most isolated stretch of highway in the country—and the shit goes downhill from there. It comes down to a matter of math: If the average road trip starts out with two carloads of five people each, and they encounter no less than two twisted psychos approximately two hundred miles into their trip, how many people return from the road trip? The answer is one, if they're lucky. So the next time your friends suggest a road trip, do yourself a favor and find a cheap flight. Yes, you may end up plummeting into the ocean or being propelled into the side of a mountain—but it will be a hell of a lot less stressful than having your road trip ruined by senseless murder.

 SCREAM QUEEN SAYS *Haven't these assholes ever heard of frequent flyer miles?*

ROAD TRIPS: THE FASTEST ROUTE TO DEATH

As the raucous drunken party is to teenage movies, the road trip is to horror films. *The Texas Chainsaw Massacre* started it. Teens who take a road trip to their grandfather's grave couldn't be expecting good results—but miraculously, these characters actually seem shocked when things take a turn for the worse.

But *TTCM* is just one of many slasher flicks in which road trips end up as a detour to hell. Some of the Scream Queen's favorites?

- *Duel* (Stephen King's first movie)
- *Wolf Creek*

- *Wrong Turn*
- *House of 1000 Corpses*
- And of course, *The Hitcher*

LISTEN TO YOUR REAL ESTATE AGENT

IN ADDITION TO THE SPACIOUS CLOSET SPACE AND HARDWOOD FLOORS, THIS HOME WITH GREAT POTENTIAL COMES WITH YOUR OWN SPAWN OF SATAN!

Once you move out of your parents' house, one undeniable truth becomes abundantly clear: it's a real bitch to find quality real estate. Whether you're renting, buying, or squatting, it's all about keeping an eye out for the right place for you. Whether that means a studio apartment in the middle of the city or a fixer-upper in the 'burbs, there's a place for everyone. Just keep your antennae up for signs that you may not be living alone. Because whenever someone in a horror movie moves into a new home, he or she barely has time to unpack before the other inhabitants of the house—usually demonic ones—make their presence known.

In *Rosemary's Baby*, small-town Rosemary and struggling actor Guy are looking for a new place to live. Excited to find a great apartment in one of Manhattan's most prestigious buildings, they are disappointed to hear a friend advise them to keep looking due to a few key oh-so-minor drawbacks about the digs. Coincidentally, the building has been the proud home to cannibals, Satanists, witches, and a man whose claim to fame was conjuring the devil. But hey, cheap rent is cheap rent, and Rosemary and Guy Woodhouse ignore their friend and their own niggling doubts and move into the apartment, excited about what the future holds. But it's not long before things start to go downhill (and not in the bursting pipes or termites kind of way).

First, Rosemary's best friend in the building is found dead, either having thrown herself or been thrown off the roof of the building. Then, there are the kind-but-overbearing neighbors, Minnie and Roman Castavets. At first, both Rosemary and Guy are grateful for the elderly couple's friendship. But Rosemary quickly grows tired of the Castavets, who elbow their way further into the Woodhouses' life. Unfortunately for her, Guy is completely enamored of them.

⚠ Rosemary becomes encouraged by their situation when Guy decides he wants to become a father—too bad the Castavets are as involved in the process as Little Guy is. Without giving away the ending, let's just say that Rosemary, for one, regrets ever moving into the apartment—especially when her baby is born looking less like Guy and more like Satan. ⚠

It's hard to blame poor Rosemary for being forced to carry the spawn of the devil—but you can question why anyone would ever move into an apartment with such a sketchy past. So if you're looking to move and someone tells you the couple next door tends to drug and forcefully rape their neighbors in hopes of giving new life to Lucifer, and may or may not push people off the tops of tall buildings, ask yourself one question: how badly do you need those new granite countertops?

 SCREAM QUEEN SAYS *You'll have a hard time enjoying those countertops when your face is repeatedly bounced off of them.*

HEED THE ADVICE OF THE LOCALS

GO BACK TO WHERE YOU CAME FROM . . . WHILE YOU STILL CAN.

It's not hard to figure out how anyone in horror movies that take place in a beyond creepy locale such as an abandoned slaughterhouse, an apocalyptic town, or a seemingly empty prison, ends up there in the first place. First off, they almost always choose the road trip (see *Reconsider That Road Trip*) as their method of travel. Then, they usually follow it with the one–two punch of getting drunk and banging each other. And nine times out of ten, they ignore the advice of freaky-ass but well-meaning locals.

Horror directors typically reserve the strangest-looking character to serve as the creepy decoy, a subtle way of challenging our assumptions. They do this with the most obvious candidate for the killer, and they certainly do it with the yokel who tries to get the unsuspecting out-of-towners to go back where they came from before it's too late. However, it's to no avail. Perhaps in thinly veiled social commentary from the moviemakers, the characters laugh off the local's advice and continue on their way into the belly of the beast. There they go, judging a weird old book by its cover, and they never quite recover. As in, they get held captive and tortured to death.

We saw this in *The Blair Witch Project*, when Heather and her small but potently obnoxious film crew ignore the advice of Scary Mary, deeming her too nuts to take seriously. We see it again in *The Shining* when Mr. Ullman, the owner of the remote inn, warns Jack that the inn can get lonely—even going as far as to recount the tale of the previous caretaker who went nuts and killed his entire family. It's a shallow but common mistake—shrugging off the advice of the crazy-looking person trying to give them an out. And serial killers don't do shallow, unless you're referring to shallow graves.

So if you're headed to someplace suspiciously sketchy where you've never been before, keep a head's up for the weird old man working at the gas station or the nutty lady when you stop to ask for directions. Don't be fooled by her lazy eye and the rusty car on her front lawn—she's just trying to help, and if she advises you *don't go any further*, I'd suggest you look her in one of her eyes, thank her, and go the hell back where you came from.

 SCREAM QUEEN SAYS *There's always that chance they're trying to lure you into a trap. But walking through each day that paranoid is no way to live.*

SURVIVAL TIP

THAT PLACE SOUND FAMILIAR IN A NOT-SO-GOOD WAY? NO NEED TO STOP AND CHECK IT OUT.

I'VE HEARD OF THIS PLACE BEFORE! IT'S THAT TOWN WHERE ALL THOSE KIDS IN THE SUMMER CAMP WERE KILLED. LET'S CHECK IT OUT!

You've heard that saying, "curiosity killed the cat." Well, maybe you'd take the warning a bit more seriously if the saying went something like, "curiosity maimed, tortured, and killed the teenager." Because that's usually what happens when someone in a horror movie decides he or she should check out a place where a horrific crime occurred.

People in horror movies are a predictable bunch. And much like they enjoy watching slasher flicks (Chapter 1), they also enjoy checking out the sites of gruesome murders. Always underestimating the seriousness of the situation, they decide they have to see the deserted town/burned-out school/ abandoned mental hospital for themselves. And while 99 percent of the time the people found guilty of the heinous crimes committed in these locations have been caught and locked up or killed, they, of course have demented relatives or devoted wives who are bound and determined to exact revenge on anyone they can blame.

In *Friday the 13th, The Final Chapter*, a bunch of undetered teenagers are fascinated by the dozens of people who were murdered just feet from where they're scheduled to stay at Crystal Lake. They proceed to rent the lake house as scheduled and it should come as abso-fuckin'-lutely no surprise that they're killed one by one. Even after death (for the third? fourth? time), Jason is unimpressed by the cavalier attitude the teens show toward his actions and picks 'em all off. While this is certainly a waste of the security deposit they put down on the house, I can't say I'm surprised. Whereas serial killers certainly appreciate admiration, they get a little freaked out by too much attention—and get really pissed off when people don't take them seriously.

 SCREAM QUEEN SAYS *Maybe that's where the phrase "crystal clear" comes from.*

MY BAD: F-UPS ON FILM: FRIDAY THE 13TH: THE FINAL CHAPTER

As you've probably noticed, almost every movie has some sort of mistake in it. Cameras visible to the audience, characters' clothes changing when they shouldn't, misspellings of names or places that are prominently featured in the film. Most of the time, they're hard to pick up on. And rarely is there a f-up so obvious that it actually takes away from the audience's enjoyment of the film. But it happens . . . as we see in *Friday the 13th: The Final Chapter.*

As Jason is happily slicing away at people (in this particular instance, Jimmy), we actually see that his cleaver has the front cut out of it to allow for Jimmy's head. Some poor prop slob obviously cut out the front of the cleaver to make the slashing more believable, but exactly the opposite was accomplished. Talk about cutting into our good time.

IF YOU HAVE ANGER ISSUES, DON'T TAKE A JOB AS CARETAKER FOR AN ISOLATED HOTEL

ALL WORK AND NO PLAY MAKE JACK A DULL BOY. ALL WORK AND NO PLAY MAKE JACK A DULL BOY. ALL WORK AND NO PLAY MAKE JACK A DULL BOY. ALL WORK AND NO PLAY MAKE JACK A DULL BOY. ALL WORK AND NO PLAY MAKE JACK A DULL BOY. ALL WORK AND NO PLAY MAKE JACK A DULL BOY. ALL WORK AND NO PLAY MAKE JACK A DULL BOY.

In the Introduction, I asked you to jog your memory to try to recall the first time you realized that you are much smarter than the average horror movie character. For me, it was the first time I watched *The Shining.*

⚠ This 1980 instant classic is one of the most terrifying movies of all time, if only because the entire movie is 100 percent believable; all the horror occurs in Jack Torrance's mind—until, of course, his mind causes him to attack his own family. ⚠️

We've all heard that we should consider our strengths when applying for a job or making a career move. Well, I can safely say that Jack (masterfully played by the creepy Jack Nicholson) didn't take his strengths and weaknesses into consideration when he agreed to accept the job as caretaker at the Overlook Hotel. He sees the time spent in the isolated mountains as a good opportunity to write his book and recuperate from his recent job loss, but we don't find out until late in the movie that he lost his job because of a violent outburst and has previously injured both his wife and son when he lost his temper while drinking. Pair the isolation of the hotel with lots of unattended booze and watch the fireworks explode.

And what the hell, may we ask, was Wendy Torrance thinking when she agreed to this work and living situation? She knew better than anyone just how, ahem, *problematic* Jack's temper could be. Yet she packed up her clairvoyant and odd little kid, whose hobbies include riding his tricycle and speaking through his index finger, and her husband, whose hobbies include drunken, violent outbursts and writing the same eerie sentence thousands of times, and headed off to no man's land.

If you're offered a job that doesn't make full use of your skill set or has the potential to drive you batshit crazy, think twice about accepting, even if it could provide you with the opportunity to get to know all those people who live inside your head.

 SCREAM QUEEN SAYS *If you start seeing a tidal wave of blood coming at you, it might be too late.*

STAY OUT OF THE CROP CIRCLES

A BIG CIRCLE IN THE CROPS! I WONDER WHO MADE IT! I WONDER WHAT THEY WOULD CALL SUCH A THING? NEVER MIND. LET'S CHECK IT OUT!

There are some places where you just know you're going to get in trouble. Karaoke bars. Your office Christmas party when the punch is dubbed "Panty-Dropping Punch" by the guy who volunteered to make it. A Focus on the Family fundraiser when you're a card-carrying member of the Democratic Party. We've discussed a few such places when it comes to horror movies: abandoned mental institutions, alien internment camps, post-apocalyptic cities. Let's add crop circles to that list, shall we?

Although not featured in a large number of horror movies, the inside of a crop circle should not be on your Places To See Before I Die List—unless you're looking to push up your expiration date by quite a bit.

⚠ In *Signs*, we see the havoc a crop circle/alien invasion can wreak on a small town in the middle of nowhere—pets and farm animals start to attack their owners, and not in an *excited to see you when you walk in the door after work* kind of way. Think about it. If crop circles can have such a bad effect on people who have no lives, what could they do to you? In *Children of the Corn*, we never learn what exactly goes on in the weird circles in the middle of the cornfield—but we do learn that no one makes it out in the same condition in which they went in. ⚠

The popular theory about crop circles is that aliens create them—and we've seen plenty of films that show us the not-so-friendly side of these otherworldly visitors. In *Alien*, it only takes about ten minutes into the movie for a little baby alien to attach itself to Kane's face—and then rip that face right off. Ouch! And even though we haven't heard about any real alien internment camps like we saw in *District 9*, I can't imagine the creatures there are any friendlier (although they have a reason, what with the internment and all).

No one knows the origin of crop circles for sure, but all "Signs" point to alien involvement . So unless you are dying to die at the hand of someone with way more limbs than you, if you see a crop circle, keep right on driving. No good can come of investigating. Besides, if you put all that time into mowing your lawn into a wicked cool shape, could anyone really blame you for punishing the people who walk on the grass?

 SCREAM QUEEN SAYS *These guys are usually more forceful than a "keep off the grass" sign.*

SURVIVAL TIP

IF SOMEPLACE SEEMS TOO GOOD TO BE TRUE, DON'T GET A HOTEL ROOM THERE

FUNNY, THE ONLINE REVIEWS DIDN'T MENTION ANYTHING ABOUT THE RITUALISTIC TORTURE. TRIPADVISOR WILL BE HEARING FROM ME!

Let's establish one thing: outside of the States, no one likes Americans. We're fat, ugly, loud, and we insist on wearing obnoxious T-shirts with the names of our cities, states, or hometown sports teams whenever we leave the country. We bitch about driving on the "wrong" side of the road, the weird toilets, and the funny-sounding food.

Okay, so these are generalizations. But the Ugly American is no myth, and this stereotype provided the basis for arguably the scariest of all the movies mentioned in this section: 2005's *Hostel*. Following two American backpackers abroad to Amsterdam, this movie is enough to scare the bejesus out of anyone who visits Europe for the reasons many Americans do: to get drunk and get lucky, preferably with hot European women. Lured to Slovakia by the promise of a hotel filled with hot, American-loving women, these young guys (truthfully, both assholes in their own loud and obnoxious American ways) want nothing more than to find someone dying to sleep with them. After a couple nights of partying and scoring with chicks way hotter than they deserve, things take a turn for the much, much worse—and not in the "my pee pee kind of burns" way.

⚠ Josh is the lucky one—his death comes near the beginning of the movie, before Paxton realizes they were lured to the hostel to be victims of a bizarre murder-for-profit business where people can pay to torture and kill people—with Americans fetching the highest price. Listen, I was as bummed as you are. Even though these guys were douchebags, it's a bit unnerving to realize that Europeans' feelings of general superiority extend to being willing to pay extra just to blast off our faces with blow torches. ⚠ So the best you can do here is take your dad's advice: be suspicious of really good deals. If someone with a snotty accent and a heightened appreciation for really good wine promises you a great deal at a hotel boasting free drinks and hot dudes, tell him you'll pass. After all, you never know who's looking to screw you. Or, to put screws in your chest.

 SCREAM QUEEN SAYS *Put away that NYPD hat, turn that Team USA T-shirt inside-out, and, for God's sake, leave the fanny pack at home.*

DON'T TRY TO HIDE

NO ONE WILL THINK TO LOOK FOR ME INSIDE THIS MEAT LOCKER!

The problem with hiding places is that they're usually dark, often cramped, and are especially hard to escape from. Yet in horror movie after horror movie, we see crafty chicks go into closets, underneath beds, and into any other small, confined space—with less than excellent results.

This is one of those damned if you do, damned if you don't situations. After all, if you don't hide, any psycho in hot pursuit will find you that much quicker. Here are a few ways you may be able to get around this Catch-22:

1. Try hiding in plain view. If you're in a horror movie or a situation that's beginning to resemble one, chances are, there are lots of bodies around. Why not throw yourself in with the rest of the carnage? If your murderous pursuer has had a busy day, he may not even realize he hasn't taken your life yet, and leave you be to stalk someone else. Or he may see you and kill you anyway. So here's a more go get 'em! technique.
2. Take the proactive approach. If you find yourself slipping into a situation that is ripe with potential for horror, try stashing weapons in the most likely hiding places ahead of time—it worked in *The Godfather*, didn't it? That way, when the killer finds your hiding spot (and he always does), you have a chance of getting him before he gets you.
3. Even a well-timed, "BOO!" when paired with jumping out of a closet has potential to throw the guy off his game.

As they say, the best defense is a good offense. Or maybe it's the best offense is a good defense. Either way, you'll sleep better at night knowing you can go on the attack if necessary. No one ever felt like a bad ass hiding underneath a bed, biting her lip, and watching the killer's feet moving around the perimeter of the bed. And though I've never experienced it firsthand, you gotta think that retrieving your well-positioned machete and slicing someone's Achilles tendons probably feels pretty good. Well, good for you, anyway.

 SCREAM QUEEN SAYS *if you can't find a machete, consider buying one of those knives that can cut a penny.*

SURVIVAL TIP

DESPITE THE LURE OF ATTENTIVE ROOM SERVICE, NEVER STAY AT A HOTEL WHERE YOU'RE THE ONLY GUEST

I THINK I MUST HAVE ONE OF THOSE FACES YOU CAN'T HELP BELIEVING.

Often regarded as the most badass horror movie ever, start to finish, Alfred Hitchcock's *Psycho* is a mind-fuck. ⚠ And one of the big reasons is that for the first third or so of the film, you think you're watching a movie about what happens when a pretty young woman destined to escape her boring life steals a bunch of money from her work—but then our heroine gets killed (before Drew Barrymore was even born). ⚠

Everyone loves Janet Leigh as the pretty but likeable Marion, yet looking back, she was a little bit of a dummy in the choice that led to her downfall: her hotel selection. Yes, this was before the days of reserving hotels online or letting

William Shatner step in as your own personal Priceline Negotiator. But I can safely say that anyone who checks into a completely empty motel should at least be suspicious as to why it's empty—especially when the owner proudly boasts that his hobbies include taxidermy (as in stuffing dead animals and hanging them on the wall).

⚠ We were all bummed when we saw Marion get stabbed to death in the shower. ⚠ But I can't say it was surprising. If you ever find yourself looking for a hotel last minute and your iPhone isn't in service, take that as a sign. After all, no matter where you stay, you should always arm yourself with one very basic form of protection: some other guests. Because if you happen to check into a hotel where the owner plans on offing somebody, at least put the odds in your favor.

 SCREAM QUEEN SAYS *Mini-bar prices will be the least of your worries.*

Alfred Hitchcock's *Psycho* has long been regarded as one of the scariest movies of all time. ⚠ And although there are many memorable scenes (our first glimpse of the Bates Hotel, Mrs. Bates' decomposing body in the rocker, Marion's car being pulled out of the swamp, and most disturbing, Norman as Mrs. Bates), what's the one that instantly comes to mind when you think of this fifty-year-old classic? The shower scene, of course. ⚠

Viewers today can't appreciate just how groundbreaking this forty-five-second scene was. Fearing lack of support from the public, Hitchcock filmed this movie in black and white so the red blood of Marion, played by Janet Leigh, wouldn't turn off mainstream viewers. In fact, that "blood" is chocolate syrup.

Despite its brevity, the shower scene took Hitchcock more than a week to film. Today, the horrifying stabbing, bone-chilling music, and Marion's screams of terror are what we remember, but back then, the censors were more concerned with the fact that the toilet is briefly visible when Marion enters the bathroom. It was the first film ever to include a shot of a toilet.

Psycho came out seventy years after live-action was first recorded . . . that's a long time to hold it.

PART 3

THE PAIN IS RELATIVE

"YOUR MOTHER ATE MY DOG."
—*DEAD ALIVE*

CHAPTER 5

IT'S A FAMILY AFFAIR

Poor Mrs. Bates—left to rot in the basement while her son enjoys taxidermy and picking off tourists just next door. Or what about Rosemary finding out that her newborn is the son of Satan? Looks like you can't trust anyone these days—not even your family.

Between overbearing parents, bratty little brothers, and your competitive (and annoyingly hotter) sister, real-life families are scary enough. But when things get horrifying, you really have to watch your back. That saying about blood being thicker than water? It so doesn't apply here.

YOU CAN'T TRUST ANYONE— NOT EVEN YOUR MOMMA

IF YOU REALLY LOVED ME, YOU WOULDN'T MIND THAT I EAT HUMAN FLESH.

She can be a bit overbearing. At times, you wish she lived far away. But hell, she's your mother! And you love her. After all, even her most annoying antics come from a place of love and the fact that she always wants what's best for you. The problem starts when what she thinks is best for you is not on par with what you had in mind. Say, for example, when she wants to kill your significant other and eat his brains.

In 1992's *Braindead* (directed by a pre-*Lord of the Rings* Peter Jackson), an overbearing character known only as "Mum" is bitten by a Sumatran Rat-Monkey while spying on her son and his date at the local zoo. Because in horror movies catching a virus can never lead to anything but turning into a zombie, Mum turns into a murderous psycho determined not only to kill her son Lionel's new girlfriend, the unfortunately named Paquita, but anyone else who crosses her path as well. Of course, Mum turns hundreds of others into zombies as well and the town is in total and utter chaos.

⚠ If you haven't seen this bizarre-o zombie flick, you should. Let's just say that zombies aren't the only things Lionel needs to worry about. He has more extreme problems, like the fact that his mom attempts to put him back into her womb even though he is a thirty-something man. Honestly, it takes the Oedipal complex to such a new level that you'll want to take a shower—and coincidentally, the characters who are still alive at the end of this film could use a shower as well. ⚠

So how do you know when you can trust your mom and when you should just ignore her for fear of getting your brains sucked out of your head—or worse? Here are a few pointers:

- If your mom tells you a particular pair of jeans makes your ass look wide, you should listen to her. After all, she's your mom and she just wants you to look your best.
- If your mom tells you she needs to drink a pint of your blood in order to keep her nourished until the mother ship arrives, you might have a problem on your hands. Give her a V8 and get the hell out of there.
- If your mom doesn't like your new boyfriend because she thinks you're above dating someone whose only career aspiration is to get a perfect score on Garage Band, you might want to take her advice and go on a blind date with that med student she met in line at the grocery store.
- If your mom doesn't like your new boyfriend and decides to eat him, you might want to talk to your dad about possibly taking her away for a relaxing weekend so poor Mum can have some downtime.
- If your mom joins you while apartment hunting and she thinks you should hold out for one that's in a safe neighborhood, consider expressing her concerns to your real estate agent.
- If your mom doesn't like the new apartment you found and suggests that you climb back into her womb where she can keep you safe, you might want to consider going back to that condo where you didn't love the kitchen but could live with the lack of counter space if you really needed to.
- If your mom doesn't think you're going to church enough, try biting the bullet and accompanying her to Mass on Sunday.

- If your mom doesn't think you're going to church enough and tries to drive a cross through your heart to show her disapproval, run.

There's no right answer when deciding when to take your mom's advice and when you're better off making your own call. But if she starts sleeping while hanging upside down and making brains on toast instead of her world-famous meatloaf, consider moving out of her basement earlier than you planned.

 SCREAM QUEEN SAYS *Zombie or not, you should still let her do your laundry when you come home for the holidays.*

MY BAD: F-UPS ON FILM: *THE AMITYVILLE HORROR*

Here's a head's up: don't move into a house that was the site of a grisly mass murder. That's exactly what the Lutz family of *The Amityville Horror* did—in both the 1979 and 2005 versions of the movie. Geez, you'd think they would have learned after the first suckers went down—but sadly, they did not.

The original version is widely regarded as the superior film, however, both versions have one thing in common: more than their share of gaffs.

In the more recent movie version of the book by Jay Anson, George and Kathy are seen driving by a Starbucks. Nothing wrong with a latte, right? Except for the fact that the story takes place in 1975, and you couldn't get a $5 half-caf caramel macchiato at our favorite fair trade coffee shop until the late 1980s.

In the earlier version of the film, Jeff is spotted driving a Jeep Cherokee with a body that wasn't available until the early 80s. The verdict here? Scary or not, these Amityville idiots needed to check their product placement.

But talk about horror: A time without Starbucks? Now that's scary.

GIVE THOSE ADOPTION PAPERS A SECOND LOOK

FUNNY, THE ADOPTION AGENCY DIDN'T MENTION YOUR TENDENCY TO EAT RAW MEAT AND TORTURE SMALL ANIMALS...

Some horror flick scenarios seem more uncalled for than others. Did Leatherface really have to pour salt on that guy's wound after cutting off his leg with a chainsaw? I'm pretty sure the whole chainsaw-to-leg thing probably stung pretty good on its own.

In *Halloween IV*, was Michael really in that big of a rush to meet and kill his favorite (now dead) victim's daughter after he awoke from his coma? Wasn't he interested in what had transpired while he was unconscious? They never told us if Michael was a big sports fan or not, but you gotta figure the guy is at least curious about who won the World Series during the past seven years.

And last but not least, is it really necessary to further upset grieving parents by giving them a son or daughter who is not the loving child they expected, but a murderous psycho dead set on killing his new family? Haven't these poor people gone through enough?

In *The Omen*, a well-intentioned but badly misinformed father tries to protect his wife by simply adopting another person's baby boy rather than telling her that she lost her baby in labor. Hey, what could go wrong, right? After all, the father did get the new baby, Damien, from a priest. Well, turns out that this "baby" is actually the Antichrist. Without giving away the end of the movie, let's just say that frogs and snails and puppy dog tails don't begin to cover what this little boy is made of. In fact, the kid was so evil, they made *The Omen II* and *III*.

In *Orphan*, we once again encounter a grieving couple looking to make up for the loss of a stillborn child by adopting a young girl named Esther. Unfortunately, the arrival of young Esther coincides with a string of tragic accidents, and when her new parents try to investigate, the adoption agency is unable to verify anything about her early childhood. Looks like it's easier to access records about a used car than it is to find out if your new child has ever exhibited signs of being a murderous psycho.

The lesson here? If you're considering adoption, go to a more reputable place than a weird old priest hanging around a hospital nursery or an adoption agency that can't figure out where they got a kid from. Apparently, even people who are willing to open their hearts to a new child are still at risk for getting said hearts cut out. Talk about taking advantage of people.

 SCREAM QUEEN SAYS *The next thing you know, there will be a new genre of horror flicks in which all the victims are elderly Peace Corps volunteers.*

DON'T HANG YOURSELF FROM THAT FAMILY TREE

BLOOD IS THICKER THAN BRAIN MATTER...

Families can be really manipulative. They guilt-trip you when you don't want to spend Christmas with them and when you'd rather spend your summer vacation at the beach with your friends than at the annual family reunion in the middle of nowhere. And those are just real-life nightmares. When it comes to horror movies, families are always making unreasonable demands of each other. They can be really overbearing—and not in that funny, *man, I've been there!* way that we see so often in romantic comedies. It's more of a do-this-for-me-or-I'll-rip-your-bowels-out-while-you're-still-alive way. Family—you can't live with 'em, can't drive a stake through their undead hearts!

There comes a time in every young girl's life when she has to question just how far she is willing to go to gain her family's approval. Are you willing to change your college major because your dad thinks you have a better chance at a career as an accountant than an art teacher? Is sacrificing your beliefs by wearing your mom's prized fur really worth it? And the biggest challenge of all—are you willing to stab your sister who has transformed into a werewolf intent on killing anyone who gets in her way?

In 2000's *Ginger Snaps*, we meet two sisters, Ginger and Brigitte, whose only true friends in life are each other. In a run of the mill, *oops, I got the tainted blood of a mutilated dog on my hands* incident, Ginger begins a transformation into a werewolf and despite the fact that she becomes a total bitch (ha!), Brigitte remains committed to finding a cure for her rapidly changing sister. Dumb. Stupid. Baaaaaad move, Brigitte.

And then there's the queen of all martyrs, Wendy Torrance of *The Shining*. Despite the fact that she knows her husband to be a violent drunk, she still decides to support him in his decision to serve as caretaker of an isolated hotel far from anyone who could help them should they run out of toilet paper or begin hallucinating and try to kill each other. We saw how her decision played out. Now that's devotion.

It's hard to resist family when they need your help. But in horror movies, there is a precedent of things going particularly badly when it comes to the fam. Far be it for you to ignore it.

 SCREAM QUEEN SAYS *Next to these freaks, even your family seems almost normal.*

SURVIVAL TIP

KEEP AN EYE ON THAT NEW STEPDAD OF YOURS

I'M NOT TRYING TO BE YOUR DAD. I JUST WANT TO BE YOUR FRIEND!

Stepmothers are the dentists of the divorced family tree. They have the reputation of being overly critical (*You should floss more! That skirt makes you look like a common prostitute!*). The word itself conjures images of chin warts and cold, judgmental eyes. But stepdads get off easy. Sure, they have the reputation for trying to be too buddy-buddy with their stepkids and it's pretty painful to witness their *Sure, you can borrow my car. Hey, I'm more like a cooler, younger uncle than a father figure* act. But horror movies have changed all that.

In both the original, 1987 version of *The Stepfather* and the far less scary 2009 remake, we see a stepfather whose M.O. goes way beyond trying to make friends with his new stepkids. The original movie introduces us to a multiple-identity serial killer who travels the country finding families in need of a husband and father. He gains the trust of a single woman and her kids, marries into said family, and then hacks them into bits before moving on to his next unlucky victims. Like many serial killers, though, this guy is a manipulative sociopath and he wins people over with his charm and good looks. That's where the suspicious teenage stepkid comes to the rescue.

In both versions of the movie, the skeptical teens are the only ones who see past the charisma of their new stepfathers. Considering half of all marriages end in divorce, it's safe to say that quite a few of you will find yourselves faced with determining whether your new, over-friendly stepparents are trying to win your trust so they can kill you—or so they can gain access to the regular sex, balanced meals, and clean laundry that marriage provides. Here's your at-a-glance guide to figuring out what you're dealing with:

- If your new stepdad insists on coming to all of your softball games, he's just being nice.
- If the coach who usually chats with your mom is found beaten to death by the home base bag, your stepdad is probably not just being nice.
- If your new stepdad lends you his car for the weekend, he's trying to win you over.
- If you find a body in the trunk, he's trying to set you up so he doesn't have to deal with you anymore. Oh, and he's a murderer.

- If your stepdad buys you a Wii, he may be trying to find something that the whole family can enjoy together.
- If he throws his nun chuck through the TV and screams, "you'll be sorry, you dirty cheating motherfucker," he's probably plotting your death.

It's never easy to fairly judge someone's true intentions when you've just met, especially when your opinion is being colored by the potential for your mother to be happier and all the new crap he's buying you. Luckily, we don't care about being fair. If you suspect that your stepdad is hiding cruel intentions, grab your mom (and your new Wii) and get the hell away from him. If it turns out you were overreacting, hey, what do you care? What were you going to do with a friend in his forties anyway?

 SCREAM QUEEN SAYS *Being forced to listen to his iPod on family trips is also grounds for escaping with your family.*

IS THAT A GUN IN YOUR POCKET? OR ARE YOU JUST ABOUT TO KILL ME?

⚠ In 1983's *Sleepaway Camp*, almost everyone ignores the Scream Queen's survival rules, the most glaring mistake being that everyone in the movie—including the movie's main character, young orphan Angela—leaves home for the summer and heads to the woods. There, the campers and staff are plagued by "accidents" including being drenched in boiling water, stung to death by bees, and hacked to pieces with an axe. ⚠ Freaky? Absolutely. But nothing too out of the ordinary for a horror movie made at the height of the slasher fad. But what was a bit out of the ordinary was the movie's ending, which is still regarded as one of the most surprising in the entire horror genre. ⚠ **Angela reveals her true identity to be that of her long-assumed dead brother, Peter—Angela was the young child who died long ago. And if that isn't surprising enough, there's Angela's method of revealing her true ID: Exposing her male genitalia to other campers and the camera.** ⚠

The Crying Game it wasn't—but you can bet more than a few tears were shed when Angela's Peter popped out.

WATCH OUT FOR ANY CLOWNS IN THE FAMILY

MAYBE YOU COULD TAKE OFF THAT RED NOSE FOR THE CHRISTMAS PICTURE?

Whoever decided that clowns are cute, fun, and appropriate for kids was one twisted mother. Either that, or he had never seen a horror movie.

In 1990's *It*, a happy-go-lucky clown named Pennywise the Dancing Clown lures children into the sewer and brutally kills them. One group of children, lovingly referred to as the Losers, fights back and believes they have killed Pennywise (also referred to as "It"). They hold on to this belief until the second half of the movie where the story picks back up with the Losers, now adults—and It back in action. To add a little bit of mystery to this already-fun scenario, a childhood bully has gone insane and is following strict orders from Pennywise to kill all the children. Now if that doesn't say loveable clown, what does? I bet his mother was proud.

But *It* isn't the only film to play on our fears of red noses and big honkin' smiles. In the very first scene of the original *Halloween*, a six-year-old Michael Myers kills his older sister, Judith, while wearing a less-goofy, more-freaky clown mask. Quite an accomplishment for someone who hasn't yet learned to write in cursive.

No one is ever thrilled when a relative announces he or she is joining the circus. But when someone in a horror movie mentions an affinity for clowns, you know that shit ain't gonna end well. So if any of your loved ones shows up at your next cocktail party wearing a Bozo wig and floppy shoes, or mentions an upcoming relocation to your town's sewer system, all I can suggest is that you find something more powerful than a whoopee cushion to fight back with.

 **SCREAM QUEEN SAYS** *Killer clowns are no laughing matter.*

SURVIVAL TIP

DON'T FORGET TO TAKE YOUR BIRTH CONTROL

THAT BUNDLE OF JOY SURE RESEMBLES A SPAWN OF SATAN.

Why anyone would ever want to have kids is beyond this Scream Queen. They're smelly, messy, dirty, they never sleep—and those are the ones who haven't been fathered by Satan. Think of the potential for things going wrong when it's Lucifer's baby gravy that gets the eggs-a-cookin'. All of a sudden, dirty diapers are the least of your worries.

As I mentioned earlier, Rosemary (played by Mia Farrow) of 1968's *Rosemary's Baby*, is thrilled when her creepy husband, Guy, decides he is ready to be a father. But she should have known right away that something was amiss when *he* told *her* that it was her ideal time to conceive. However, things were different back then and perhaps in those days even ovulation cycles were left up to the men. After all, Mia hadn't been screwed over by Woody yet so she didn't have reason to write off the entire sex like she did after he married their adopted daughter. So Rosemary agreed that night it would be.

Unfortunately for Rosemary, Guy has made a pact with the devil, which involves letting the Prince of Darkness pinch hit for him. Those horror stories you've heard about aching backs, swollen feet, and bad skin are nothing compared to the pregnancy symptoms Rosemary endures, including sharp pains, exhaustion, and craving raw meat—not to mention the fact that she looks like total hell and told her friends it felt like the baby was trying to claw its way out of her. Ahh, the glow of pregnancy.

⚠️ The one way Rosemary does luck out is that after she accepts the baby as her own (even giving him the name she and her husband once daydreamed about), presumably, she kicks Guy to the curb without having to worry about paternal rights—since her baby daddy is actually Satan himself. ⚠️

 SCREAM QUEEN SAYS *I bet that bastard didn't even pay child support.*

BEWARE OF BADLY BEHAVED BROTHERS

I'M SORRY YOU HAD TO WEAR HAND-ME-DOWN GIRL'S PAJAMAS GROWING UP . . . DOES THAT WARRANT A STABBING?

Brothers are bad enough in real life. Growing up, they constantly bug you and mess with your stuff. You're either stuck with their decidedly unfeminine hand-me-downs or are forced to share your toys with them. Later, they always try to sleep with your friends—and sometimes, your friends actually have the bad taste to go for it! And, as if that wasn't horrifying enough, in the movies, those pesky little fuckers can really ruin your life. You know . . . by ending it.

We've already covered the World's Worst Little Brother, that creepy little shit Michael Myers. It wasn't bad enough that he watched his older sister do the nasty, then he had to go and stab her for it. That makes banging one of your friends look downright civilized.

⚠️ In *Scream 3*, Sidney Prescott barely even knew she had a brother for five minutes before that jerk tried to kill her. Turns out her mom had an affair and gave birth to the bastard almost thirty years previously without Sidney ever knowing. ⚠️ That introduces quite a few pieces of bad news to poor Sidney:

1. You have a brother you never knew about.
2. He killed your mother and most of your friends.
3. Now he's going to try to kill you.
4. Your mom was a slut.

It's true that sisters are no picnic, but brothers have a special way of screwing up their sisters' lives—especially in horror movies. So if you're lucky enough to just have chicks in your family or, better yet, be an only child, count your blessings. You gotta figure it increases your chances of not having to share your car—and the odds of living to see your twenty-first birthday.

 SCREAM QUEEN SAYS *A life with brothers is no life at all—especially if that asshole is just going to kill you.*

SURVIVAL TIP

NEVER TRY TO COME BETWEEN SISTERS

YOU AND YOUR SISTER HAVE THE SAME EYES . . . YOUR TAILS LOOK ALIKE, TOO!

If you have a sister, you know how unbreakable that bond is. True, you may fight like cats and dogs, but you know that you'll also be the first to take out anyone who dares to mess with your sister. And by "take out" I mean verbally bashing and berating—unless we're talking about the sisters in horror movies. When it comes to bashing, those broads go for the head—so do yourself a favor and stay the hell out of it.

The craziest and best bond between horror sisters has to be that of Ginger and Brigitte in 2000's *Ginger Snaps.* Even before the real scary stuff goes down, the two already share a freaky bond. Not only are they Canadian, but they also spend their time fantasizing about ways they may kill themselves if life in their Podunk town doesn't pick up. Well, pick up it does.

After accidentally becoming infected with tainted dog blood, Ginger begins a transformation to a werewolf. Brigitte, determined to stand by her sister despite the change, ends up the unwilling accomplice to several of Ginger's werewolf-type crimes, such as accidentally killing one of their friends, a few of her teachers, and purposefully infecting a guy with the werewolf germ. Despite Brigitte's horror at Ginger's crimes, she remains committed to curing Ginger of her werewolfitis. One of the two sisters actually makes it out of the movie alive—but not before a long and bloody battle ensues between the two.

Many of the people who got offed in *Ginger Snaps* were, unfortunately, reduced to very dead collateral damage in the fight between Ginger and Brigitte. If you find yourself around a pair (or worse! more than a pair) of fighting sisters—especially if they're prepared to kill each other—stay far, far away. In the end, sisters always stick together. And if that means cutting you into bits and stuffing you in their freezer, well, somebody better move the frozen peas because you're going on ice.

 SCREAM QUEEN SAYS *Werewolves or not, anyone who gets between sisters is going to end up howling for help.*

SURVIVAL TIP

IF YOUR DAD CLAIMS HE'S RECEIVED A CALLING FROM GOD, TELL HIM TO TAKE A MESSAGE

I HAD A VISION GOD SENT US TO ERADICATE DEMONS ... BUT FIRST I WANT YOU TO TAKE OUT THE TRASH AND CLEAN THE GARAGE.

Everyone's dad embarrasses them at some time in their lives. Whether he asks every guy you bring home about wedding plans or walks around in tighty-whities while you're hosting a sleepover, dads can be quite the cross to bear. But things could always be worse, as 2001's *Frailty* reminds us.

The movie focuses on two brothers, Fenton and Adam, and their dad, all three of whom are grieving the recent loss of the boys' mother. Unfortunately for the boys, Dad gets a late night communication from God, which commands Dad, Fenton, and Adam to do God a solid and wipe out a list of "demons," whose names God has thoughtfully provided. Fenton immediately recognizes that Dad is a loon, but Adam finds nothing wrong with aiding dear old Dad in a dozen or so murders, building a dungeon in their backyard, and discouraging Fenton from ratting them out.

Much like Judge Judy's courtroom, justice is not guaranteed in horror flicks and in *Frailty*, poor Fenton ends up in the dungeon himself. Seems the whole mess could have been avoided if he had sought help as soon as Dad gave the news about IMing with Jesus.

Hey, you didn't fall for his bullshit when your dad tried to convince you that a road trip to the Basketball Hall of Fame would be more fun than renting the beach house from *Jersey Shore* for a weekend. So why wouldn't you call him out on his crap when he tried to recruit you for his evil mission from God? He forgave you for telling your friends that you were an orphan just so you wouldn't have to introduce him during his unfortunate moustache phase. He'll eventually get over you turning him into the cops—especially if he wants you to be his right-hand man as he carries out God's not-so-good work.

 SCREAM QUEEN SAYS *There's always the possibility he'll ground you . . . but it's hard to follow through from the looney bin.*

HORROR WHERE YOU LEAST EXPECT IT: PEE-WEE'S BIG ADVENTURE

For any child of the '80s, Pee-wee's Big Adventure was a big deal. A big screen version of everyone's favorite Saturday morning TV show, the movie follows Pee-wee (played by everyone's favorite public masturbator, Paul Reubens) as he goes on a road trip to find his beloved bike, which has been stolen.

We see this man-child as he makes his way across the country, bound and determined to get his ten-speed back. Pee-wee makes more than a few mistakes—not the least of which is accepting a ride from a trucker named Large Marge. As she drives Pee-wee to his next destination, she begins to tell him a story of "the worst accident that I've ever seen!" that just so happened on the stretch of highway they're driving along. Pee-wee becomes visibly agitated, beginning to consider how he can get out of the truck as soon as possible.

As Marge pulls up to a diner, she concludes her story by revealing that she herself was involved in the car crash—and she shows her skeletal face, complete with eyes leaping out of their sockets, before she leaves Pee-wee by emphatically saying, "Tell 'em Large Marge sentcha!" Later, Pee-wee is freaked to all hell to learn that Large Marge was in fact killed in the accident she described.

Doesn't sound so scary, right? After all, getting a ride from a ghost with a mutilated face is pretty par for the course when we're talking horror movies. The scary thing is, the movie was rated a family-friendly PG, and effectively scared the Underoos off a whole generation of little kids. What did you expect from a kid's movie directed by Tim Burton?

NUTTY OR NICE, BE KIND TO YOUR MOTHER

SHE GAVE YOU THE GIFT OF LIFE ... AND SHE CAN TAKE IT RIGHT BACK.

There are a few undeniable truths in life. First, as soon as you begin to think you know someone, he'll surprise you. Second, there are two sides to every story. Third, beer before liquor, never been sicker; liquor before beer, you're in the clear. And finally, always be nice to your mother—even in horror movies.

True, the moms of horror movies aren't the same type of mothers we know and love. You'll never see a horror movie mom driving her kids to soccer practice or running around before the holidays, making sure each of her children receives the exact same number of Christmas presents. But that rule about being nice to her stands nonetheless.

The consequences of not getting along with your mother in real life are different than in horror movies, too. In real life, for example, you may find yourself riddled by phone calls from your mom at all hours of the night, her lame attempt to make you feel guilty for not spending more time with her. But in horror movies such as *Carrie*, you may find yourself locked in the closet by your psychotic mother, her lame attempt to make you feel guilty for getting your period for the first time.

The way a girl shows appreciation for her mom in real life is also different in horror flicks. In real life, you may bring your mom flowers on her birthday and Mother's Day to show her you care (and to avoid a serious guilt trip). In a horror movie, you may keep your mom's rotting body in the basement and wear her underwear every once in a while to show her how much you miss her. Hey, who are we to judge? Few things in life are more complicated than the relationship between a mother and her child.

Though the mothers of the horror genre may be, well, horrifying and undeserving of love from their offspring, they tend to be a crazy bunch. Whether they're driven gonzo by grief or are just plain old inexplicably bonkers, horror moms are capable of some bizarre behavior. So it serves you well to be nice to these batty bitches. After all, if normal mothers are capable of extreme outbursts of anger (and we've all been on the receiving end of some maternal rage), you'll want to keep those insane mothers on your good side.

 SCREAM QUEEN SAYS *When the horror moms are around, you're in for a motherf***ing nightmare.*

CHAPTER 6

THAT'S ONE F***ED-UP LITTLE KID

Everyone loves a cute kid, especially when that little ankle-biter is someone else's responsibility. But what happens when the little bastard next door turns out to be undead—and wants to make the same arrangements for you?

You've got a scary kid on your hands. Although popular culture doesn't condone wiping out children left and right, some of horror's most disturbing little brats are enough to make you second-guess your after-school babysitting job.

DON'T LET YOUR SON RIDE HIS TRICYCLE INDOORS

EVERY LITTLE BOY NEEDS A TRICYCLE. UNLESS HE'S CREEPY.

The image of a sweet little child riding on his brand new tricycle is one that many people conjure when daydreaming about the son they may have one day. Unfortunately for them, horror movies have turned this little slice of Americana into a potentially disturbing nightmare—thanks to two of the creepiest little dudes to ever grace the big screen. Although the ways they make your skin crawl vary greatly, Damien Thorn and Danny Torrance are undeniably two of the most spinetingly, eerie kids in horror history.

Damien (of *The Omen* series), while attempting to keep the true nature of his identity a secret, brings a series of bad accidents upon his family and all those around him.

⚠ Oh, screw it. Anyone who hasn't seen *The Omen* or at least heard the premise of this movie must live under a rock anyway. Damien is the Antichrist and his mission seems to be to kill everyone he comes across. ⚠

Danny is pure of heart—but he occasionally slips into the persona of Tony, a little boy whom Danny claims lives in his mouth, talks through his finger, and has the voice of a seventy-year-old woman who smokes a pack of Misty Slims before she gets out of bed every morning. Oh, and there is that little ability to communicate with his mind.

These two creepy little kids both spend a good amount of time getting into mischief while on their tricycles. Damien uses his to knock his mother over a railing, causing her to lose her unborn child. (God forbid the poor woman would have one kid who didn't come with a tattoo of 666 on the back of his dome.) Danny explores The Overlook Hotel on his trike—and ends up quite literally opening the door to his father's mental breakdown. You gotta figure that these weird kids wouldn't have gotten into trouble quite as quickly if they were forced to rely on their five-year-old feet to get them around.

No matter how you slice it, letting a kid ride his tricycle in the house is never going to end well. Even if he doesn't send you flying over a banister or open the door to your mental breakdown, he's probably going to end up breaking Grandma's crystal or hurting himself when he crashes into the wall. Why not give your kid something a bit less sinister than a tricycle, like a hippity-hop or some old-fashioned roller skates? There's no way even a jaded mind like mine could twist a kid bouncing on a huge ball with handles into anything other than a kid playing on his hippity-hop—but the potential for damage to your house still stands.

 SCREAM QUEEN SAYS *Statistically speaking, you're better off with daughters.*

STEER CLEAR OF CREEPY CHILDREN WHO TALK TO (OR OF) GHOSTS
I SEE DEAD PEOPLE.

True, not every kid in horror movies is bad. Danny Torrance's only crime was talking through his finger and riding his tricycle indoors. And that disturbing little kid from *The Ring* was just an innocent victim of a straight-to-video art house movie. But if kids from slasher flicks have taught us anything, it's this: when a creepy, soft-spoken child pops up every time you turn around, trouble's not far behind.

So what do you do if you suspect the eight-year-old next door is either a serial killer or a warning of freaky things to come? Start small.

First off, try taking the kid for a spray tan. True, it's not the time to consider vanity. But have you ever seen an evil child with a skin tone that suggests anything but mid-February in Wisconsin? Some exfoliator and a bronze glow will give even the most evil child something to smile about.

Next, why not treat the kid to an ice cream? Maybe it wouldn't have been necessary to drown the meowing boy in *The Grudge* if someone had taken him for a double scoop with sprinkles. Who has the energy to pursue vengeance against the ghost inhabiting your house when you're battling brain freeze?

When all else fails, pack your stuff and move. Sure, you may have problems selling your house with all the cat carcasses around, but it will be well worth it when your biggest concern about your neighbors is that their dog pees on your front lawn.

 SCREAM QUEEN SAYS *Shot through the heart and Damien's to blame. Pale little bastards give kids a bad name.*

MY BAD: F-UPS ON FILM

Halloween (1978) took place in an Illinois suburb. However, all the cars in the film have California license plates—and this is only one of the many mistakes in the movie. In one scene, Laurie (played by the woman who resurrected the term "Scream Queen," Jamie

Lee Curtis) says, "He's right out there." The line was supposed to be said by her friend, Lindsey, who in fact goes on to say it. True, these gaffs add to the film's charm—but they also cause a distraction and take you out of the moment when viewing them.

FIND A BETTER HIDING SPOT FOR THE VIDEOS YOU DON'T WANT YOUR KIDS TO FIND

I'LL JUST LEAVE THIS DVD IN THE DVD PLAYER . . . HE'LL NEVER FIND IT HERE!

Everyone thinks their friends' parents are cooler, better parents than their own—and that is never truer than when a kid accidentally stumbles upon a naughty video belonging to her mom, dad, or worst of all, starring her mom and dad.

It's as important as any other lesson in life—parents should always hide their porn really, *really* well. Your child's happiness depends on it. No one wants to think about her mom or dad in that way. Equally important to keep hidden? A video you think may kill everyone who views it within one week.

In 2002's *The Ring*, a young single mother and journalist, Rachel Keller, is investigating the existence of a VHS (for the young ones, a VHS is like a DVD, only fatter and you have to rewind it) that she thinks may somehow be tied to her niece's sudden death. Through her research, she finds a copy of the tape and, after watching it, determines that everyone who watches the tape indeed dies within a week. In case that wasn't a dumb enough move, Rachel then leaves the tape in the VCR (machine that plays the fat DVDs), only to have her young son find and watch the tape. Now they're both f'd.

Like that of a kid who finds his dad's porn collection, Rachel's son's life becomes unnecessarily stressful and complicated after watching the video. So take a lesson from not-so-bright Rachel. Any video you don't want your kid to see—whether it is a homemade adult movie or a grainy VHS that holds the potential to end your life in a sudden and violent manner—should be hidden in a really, really good spot.

 SCREAM QUEEN SAYS *If you end up finding a video your parents don't want you to see, you'll wish you could rewind in real life.*

SURVIVAL TIP

AVOID CHILDREN WITH OLD SOULS

ALTHOUGH I FIND YOUR KNOWLEDGE OF FOREIGN POLICY QUITE PECULIAR FOR A SIX-YEAR-OLD, I MUST ADMIT, IT'S NICE TO HAVE SOMEONE WITH WHOM I CAN PARTAKE IN INTELLIGENT DISCOURSE.

It's so cute when a young child says or does something that seems bizarrely adult-like. At one time or another, every parent watches her kid and thinks to herself, "My God, when did she get so grown up?" Pity if it that moment occurs when you watch your son or daughter brutally kill someone.

In 2009's *Orphan*, a couple adopts nine-year-old Esther and quickly becomes impressed by her superior intelligence and maturity . . . that is, until it starts to freak them the fuck out. Even before she breaks a classmate's ankle, bludgeons a nun with a hammer, frames her adoptive mother as a lapsed alcoholic, attempts to seduce her new father, and threatens to kill both of her new siblings, her new parents are suspicious of her skill at the piano and advanced knowledge of sex. ⚠ She is unlike any nine-year-old they have ever seen . . . which makes sense when they discover that Esther is not a young girl at all, but is in fact a thirty-three-year-old woman with a rare disease that prevents her from aging. You'd think the name "Esther" would have tipped them off. ⚠

Sure, some young kids just seem old (like that little Manny kid in *Modern Family*). But, until you're 100 percent sure that they're not suffering from a made-up horror movie disease, keep an eye out for any extreme adult-like behavior, such as manipulation and murder.

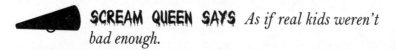 **SCREAM QUEEN SAYS** *As if real kids weren't bad enough.*

THE GLARINGLY BAD

In 1997, a dark time fell over the horror community. Against all reason and logic, Stephen King allowed a miniseries to be made of his bestselling novel, and already blockbuster movie, *The Shining*.

Start to finish, it was a total nightmare—and not in the way the original was. Bad acting paired with modern plot twists and the limitations of filming for TV combined to make one of the crappiest miniseries ever. And remember, good things have come out of made-for-TV horror—remember *It*?

According to long-circulated rumors parts of both the original film version of *The Shining* and the travesty TV version were filmed in Maine. Unfortunately/luckily for Maine's reputation as a solid place to film horror flicks, the original was actually filmed in England and Oregon; the miniseries was filmed in the state where King found his original inspiration for the novel, Colorado.

The only thing scarier than the great state of Maine is trying to make an updated version of a classic. And I'm not just talking about horror flicks. No, this problem exists in all genres. Just look at how the new 90210 turned out. Now that's some horrifying shit.

INVESTIGATE COINCIDENCES
IT'S A GOOD THING YOU'RE ALWAYS AROUND WHEN THESE ACCIDENTS OCCUR SO YOU CAN TELL US WHO IS REALLY TO BLAME.

We all know adults who seem to get away with anything and everything. You know the type—she never gets more than a warning when she's pulled over for speeding, always gets an extra order of fries thrown in with her burger, neighbors don't complain when she parks on their front lawn. In horror movies, there's one surefire way to escape suspicion, even when someone is guilty as sin—just be a young child, and the world is your (bloody, bludgeoned) playground.

The kid who got away with the most in all of horror history has to be Damien. The kid is the freaking spawn of the devil, is always around when a terrible accident occurs, and yet somehow he ends up getting his adopted father blamed for the series of deaths that have followed him. That kid could fall and he would land in a puddle of money, or something else demons consider even more valuable. Damien's not the only creepy kid who gets away with murder, either. In 1974's *The Devil Times Five*, not even a bathtub full of piranhas is enough to convince people that a group of young kids deserves the axe. And in 1993's *The Good Son*, a ten-car pile-up isn't enough to convince adults that young Henry is one twisted brother.

Learn from the mistakes of these easily fooled adults who didn't realize what they were dealing with until it was way too late. If your annoying nephew is always around when things go wrong, you might want to tell your sister that her kid could be the son of Satan. And that aggravating little girl next door who has seen no less than three of her kittens die in as many years? Try telling her parents just how concerned you are about the possibility that their kid is mutilating animals. Sure, most of the time, you'll end up looking like a paranoid psycho. But if it turns out that you're right and you do have a bad seed on your hands, you'll be the hero of the day.

 SCREAM QUEEN SAYS *Proceed with caution. The truth sometimes hurts and people don't always respond well when accused of raising sadistic murderers.*

SURVIVAL TIP

NEVER BABYSIT

FIGHTING FOR YOUR LIFE IS HARDLY WORTH TEN BUCKS AN HOUR.

Babysitting is a real bitch, even when a murderous stalker isn't involved. Underpaid and overworked, the very least you can hope for is to end your night without any vomit or butt wiping—and you're rarely so lucky. Add in the fact that you're basically alone in a near-stranger's house, and you have all the fixings for your own little piece of hell.

The scariest of all babysitting horror movies is 1979's *When a Stranger Calls.* ⚠ The cliché line "The call is coming from inside the house!" originated in this movie, which depicts a young girl plagued by increasingly threatening prank calls as she babysits—only to find out that the calls are being made from the same house where she is sitting and that her two young charges have been murdered in their beds. ⚠ Despite the fact that the killer is captured before the babysitter, Jill, can be injured, he manages to escape from an asylum seven years after the murders and makes a beeline for Jill. As if one night of babysitting isn't enough punishment.

In the original *Halloween*, seventeen-year-old Laurie is stalked as she babysits for her young neighbor on the scariest holiday of the year, which also happens to be the anniversary of the Michael Myers murder. He, too, has escaped from an institution. Seems like the 1970s were not well known for the tight security of state-fun facilities.

In 2008's *Babysitter Wanted*, it's the parents that young babysitter Angie has to look out for. Seems they'll do anything for their son, Sam, who has a very particular diet— which Angie is doomed to become too familiar with.

Hey, everyone needs money. But there are few professions more dangerous than babysitting. If you're considering taking up babysitting, thinking you'll just watch movies and eat junk food while the kids sleep, try Googling the phrase "Babysitter killed"—but only if you have time to read the 2 million search results.

 SCREAM QUEEN SAYS *If you really need the cash, try a safer job, like shark cage tester or guard at a 1970s mental institution.*

MY BAD: F-UPS ON FILM: *SCREAM*

In 1996's *Scream*, the character Randy points out the three most obvious rules of horror movies (the old sex and drinking rules), and ends with, "Don't say I'll be right back, because you won't." The characters who break the rules are, of course, killed. However, at the end of the film, Gale is left standing—despite the fact that she very pointedly told Kenny, "I'll be right back."

In a movie based on revealing the stereotypes and ridiculousness of horror films, this is a glaring error that should leave viewers wondering how the filmmakers let this one go. It could be that Courteney Cox Arquette's mid-90s star power was just too good to leave her out of the sequel . . . but any Scream Queen knows that if the four magic words are uttered, the next sound we should hear is the SPLAT of blood.

SURVIVAL TIP

TAKING PART IN AN EXPERIMENTAL DRUG TRIAL? YOU'RE NOT THE ONLY ONE YOU MAY BE MESSING UP

WHAT BAD COULD COME OF PUMPING MY BODY FULL OF DRUGS I KNOW NOTHING ABOUT?

We've already been over the fact that the horror movie industry does not look kindly upon people who take drugs. If 1984's *Firestarter* means anything, that dislike of drugs is not limited to the recreational kind.

Proof that drugs will mess you up in more ways than you can imagine, *Firestarter*'s Andy takes part in a government-sponsored drug trial that leaves him able to auto-hypnotize people, gives his wife telepathic abilities (the first and only time that mind reading qualifies as an STD), and curses his young daughter, Charlie, with a pyrokinetic ability.

Realizing they are to blame for the family's strange gifts, the government kills Andy's wife and pursues Charlie and her father, determined to make use of their special powers. Unfortunately for them, Charlie definitely qualifies as one f***ed up little kid. Whenever she gets angry, Charlie uses her mind to set fire to whatever or whoever is disturbing her—and the government agents who want to capture her and perform experiments on her? Well, it's fair to say they qualify as someone who disturbs her. The whole movie is like one big weenie roast.

Few sights are more disturbing than a six-year-old girl setting people and places on fire without a moment's hesitation—and you should remember that if you ever feel tempted to take part in one of those paid drug trials. Yes, the possibility of pocketing a few hundred dollars for very little work is alluring, but not only could you mess up your own life, you could also burden your unborn kids with the curse of setting people on fire whenever they get vaguely PO'd.

 **SCREAM QUEEN SAYS** *Think about how hard that will make the first day of middle school.*

PART 4

GIVING A WHOLE NEW MEANING TO THE TERM "BACK STABBERS"

"YOU KNOW WHAT? YOU WERE NEVER REALLY A GOOD FRIEND. EVEN WHEN WE WERE LITTLE, YOU USED TO STEAL MY TOYS. . ."
"AND NOW, I'M EATING YOUR BOYFRIEND. SEE? AT LEAST I'M CONSISTENT."
—JENNIFER'S BODY

CHAPTER 7

KEEP YOUR FRIENDS CLOSE (AND CHOP YOUR ENEMIES INTO BITS)

Leatherface, Freddie, and Jason aren't exactly good guys, you have to admit—they put it all out there right from the start. They make it easy for you by wearing a hockey mask and carrying a chainsaw while running errands. They never try to pass themselves off as the caring best friend, amiable new stepfather, or sympathetic boyfriend. But, in most cases, although it's terribly inconvenient, if you want to survive a horror movie, you need to question everyone—including your trusty sidekick and devoted boyfriend. Sometimes, the only prayer you have is to keep your friends close and chop your enemies into bits.

IF YOUR HUSBAND OR BOYFRIEND IS CLEANING UP WITHOUT YOUR ASKING (OR OTHERWISE BEING EXCEPTIONALLY NICE), BE AFRAID—VERY AFRAID

TAKING OUT THE TRASH AGAIN? YOU'RE SO THOUGHTFUL . . .

Picture this . . .

You get home tired after a long day at work, happy to be home but not looking forward to your nightly ritual of neatening up the house before you start preparing dinner. But before you even shut the door behind you, the smell of food hits your nostrils. *Strange*, you think to yourself, *I don't remember leaving explicit instructions to cook dinner, along with the instructions as to where the ingredients can be found.*

Pausing to set down your purse, you notice that the gigantic pile of shoes that normally clutters your doorway has been reduced to half the usual number, and the ones that remain are in a tidy row. Now you're scared.

Cue eerie music . . . As you walk into the kitchen, your eye is drawn to the trashcan, which, quite alarmingly, is not about to overflow but seems to have been emptied recently. Next to the kitchen sink, bare and gleaming, sits a dish rack of freshly washed dishes. Your boyfriend is at the stove, carefully stirring a pot of homemade marinara. Sensing your presence, he looks up and hands you a glass of wine. "Welcome home!"

See what's wrong with this picture? In real life, this scenario means that:

1. It's your birthday or anniversary.

2. He has bad news, like he cheated on you or dropped your grandmother's wedding ring down the garbage disposal.
3. He's gay.

In horror movies, it's even worse. Whenever a boyfriend or husband starts behaving perfectly:

1. He has recently murdered someone and is planning to murder you.
2. He is actually not your boyfriend at all, but a pod person.
3. He poisoned the food he's about to serve you.

Any way, it's a scary situation.

⚠️ You can accuse me of making gender stereotypes if you'd like, but the proof is on the DVD. In 1978's *Invasion of the Body Snatchers*, Elizabeth wakes up one weekend morning to find her boyfriend dressed and alert, cleaning their bedroom and taking out the trash. Therefore, it was no surprise when we found out he was no longer Geoffrey, but an alien who had taken over Geoffrey's body.

In *Scream*, as soon as Sidney's boyfriend starts being extra nice to her, she finds out that he has been on a murderous rampage for weeks and—surprise!—he killed her mother. And in *Rosemary's Baby*, when Guy pretends to want a baby, what he actually wants is to bring a spawn of Satan to earth. ⚠️

In the endless search for a nice guy, you should be aware of those who are too nice to you. They're either scheming to sleep with your roommate or to tie up and kill your entire family. Either way, your next holiday would be ruined. So keep your expectations realistic—and if he starts cleaning without asking and otherwise acting crazy, you better give him the "let's just be friends" talk (over the phone, while you're someplace far away and safe) and stay the hell away from him.

SCREAM QUEEN SAYS *If he wants to talk about your feelings, you know you have a real sociopath on your hands.*

CHECK REFERENCES

THE HAND THAT ROCKS THE CRADLE IS THE ONE THAT ARRANGES FOR YOU TO BE SLIVERED IN A GREENHOUSE ACCIDENT.

Whether you're selling an old bureau on Craigslist or looking for a housekeeper, these days it's easier than ever to end up with an unhinged lunatic in your house without you even knowing it. In *The Hand That Rocks the Cradle*, we saw a couple (Michael and Claire) end up on the verge of divorce, attacked with a sledgehammer, and nearly bludgeoned with a fireplace poker—all because they failed to notice a few key things upon their first meeting with Peyton (played by Rebecca De Mornay), including:

- Peyton Flanders is the most half-assed alias ever. There has never been a name that sounded less real.
- Their new nanny closely resembled the hooker that Tom Cruise banged on a subway car in *Risky Business.*
- They were living a horror cliché: they trusted someone who was going to be living in their house without ever checking her references.

Yes, the sadly moronic couple lived in a day before Google (shudder). However, this broad's face had been splashed on the cover of every major newspaper in the city, revealing her as the widow of a man whose life Claire ruined by identifying him as a yuckier-than-usual girl parts doctor. While unfortunate, the couple's experience with the nanny was far from unpredictable—it's common knowledge that grief-driven murderers are well known for their above average looks and unreliable résumés. So if you're hiring someone for a job that involves sharing a bathroom, do your homework—get on Facebook and see if you can find this person who's clamoring to be your underpaid employee. If she doesn't exist in the name listed on her résumé, well, then, this person is a murderer. End of story.

 SCREAM QUEEN SAYS *Thank you so much for coming in today. We'll be in touch if we're interested!*

SURVIVAL TIP
AVOID EXCESSIVE POPULARITY
`HOW COULD YOU POSSIBLY KILL ME? DON'T YOU KNOW HOW MANY FACEBOOK FRIENDS I HAVE?!`

Some people hold the 'tude that second place is the first loser. That may be true in most cases. But when it comes to horror movies, second-best is good enough. In fact, that red ribbon may be the reason you get to keep that pretty head of yours.

In high school slasher flicks, the worst possible situation to be in is most popular. Prom queens, football captains, and head cheerleaders always end up with their heads on platters. ⚠ We know how things turned out for the prom king in *Carrie*—bloody and burned up, thanks in no part to a very vengeful and jealous group of teens including a young John Travolta. In *I Know What You Did Last Summer*, beauty queen Helen is iced and then put on ice. In *Slaughter High*, the most popular students play a nasty trick on one of the nerdiest kids in their class, only to end up regretting their actions when he goes psycho on them. In fact, in any horror movie, it's hard to remember even one character of average social rank. And unlike high school, it's a good thing to be forgettable in a horror movie— it usually means your death scene wasn't especially disturbing. So how do you avoid the curse of popularity? Be sure to avoid any and all of the following:

- impossibly shiny hair which you never wear in a ponytail
- taking part in any competition that involves a crown
- being the "captain," "head," or "president" of any club, unless it's a really nerdy one
- dating the captain, head, or president of anything
- regularly hosting parties that a large number of people attend
- surrounding yourself with good-looking people who are slightly less good-looking than you are

While it's hard to resist the lure of popularity, especially in those all-important high school years, slasher flicks teach us that middle of the road is the way to go. Too nerdy, you get driven crazy by bullies and often end up dead in the fracas. Too popular, and you become the target of some not-so-great attention. But those kids in the middle fly right below the radar and make it out of their teenage years alive. Which, when you think about it, is pretty much the best you can hope for from high school.

SCREAM QUEEN SAYS *Even if the popular kid doesn't get killed, history teaches us she'll drop out of college and wind up in a loveless marriage.*

KEEP THAT TIME OF THE MONTH TO YOURSELF

THEY DON'T CALL IT THE CURSE FOR NOTHING!

Certain things in life should remain private, even between the closest of friends. Nose picking. Bathing suit shopping. And at the top of that list? Getting your period.

Most of us don't have any trouble keeping that monthly annoyance to ourselves. Yet in horror movies, it's an unreasonably public affair. The most famous instance of a girl getting her period is, of course, the opening scene in *Carrie*. Clueless about her own bodily functions because of her repressed childhood, Carrie White unfortunately gets her first period in the locker room after gym class. Her always supportive classmates proceeded to peg her with what seems like an entire drugstore aisle worth of cotton ammo, rather than letting poor Carrie in on what the rest of us found out through a poorly acted video shown in fourth grade health class.

Less famous but equally disturbing is the scene in *Ginger Snaps* in which the title character's first period coincided with her being attacked by a werewolf (and that's not one of my clever plays on words—we're talking a literal attack here). For Ginger, the day a girl becomes a woman (at least that's what most of our mothers lamely called it) turned into the day she became a werewolf.

In the old days, girls used to be sequestered during their periods, deemed unfit to interact with the rest of society—and we all know a few chicks we'd like to shun during their special time. That's probably not necessary, but during your least favorite week of the month, try laying low, especially if you're in a horror movie scenario. Steer clear of public showers, keep that werewolf at arm's length, and try not to let your hormonal mood swing drive you to murderous rage. After all, no one wants to hear about it anyway.

 **SCREAM QUEEN SAYS** *And you thought PMS was a bitch.*

STEER CLEAR OF SMALL-TOWN LAW ENFORCEMENT

I'M GOING TO HAVE TO ASK YOU TO STEP OUT OF THE VEHICLE, MAN IN THE HOODED SWEATSHIRT WITH A MACHETE IN HIS HAND.

Police officers in small towns just can't get a break. They sign up for the job hoping to serve and protect the inhabitants of a Podunk town, most of whom they probably went to high school with. What they end up doing is breaking up underage drinking parties, interrupting kids doing the nasty in the back of their parents' cars, offering rides home to drunks, and putting up with the ridicule of the very same jackasses they signed on to look out for. Even when they do see some action, things tend to turn out badly for them—especially in horror movies.

Halloween. Scream. Silent Hill. Jeepers Creepers. Even when the poor cops in these movies didn't actually die (and most of them did), none of them had a particularly good run. In fact, the scene in *Jeepers Creepers* where the killer eats a police officer's tongue is enough to scare me out of ever considering a career in law enforcement. These poor guys can't be expected to help us should a horror flick situation ever arise—in fact, it seems their presence actually increases the chances that we'll end up getting offed. So while it's unlikely that you'll be able to call for help (thanks to that unreliable cell service and that piece of shit car of yours), it turns out that hey! even if you do, guess what—you're still screwed.

Maybe, if you find yourself in a situation where you're facing down a brutal killer who wants your head, instead of trying fruitlessly to save your ass, what you should do is appeal to his "damn the man!" 'tude and try to establish some common ground. Instead of the ubiquitous and ineffective, "Why are you doing this?" paired with a girly scream and a heavy sob, maybe you should tell him about the time you dumped trash on the front lawn of the police station. Or the Halloween when you threw eggs at a passing cruiser. Maybe he'll appreciate your go-get-'em spirit and take mercy on you. After all, unless you are related to a police officer in a small jurisdiction, you probably don't like the fuzz anymore than he does (although, presumably, your indiscretions are on a smaller scale). Although no one likes a speed trap, it's hardly worth shooting a cop with his own gun to avoid the $40 ticket.

 **SCREAM QUEEN SAYS** *A nightstick will only do someone so much good.*

WHERE DID THE DUDE IN THE BACKSEAT COME FROM?

The Killer in the Backseat is an urban legend that dates back to ancient times—movie historians have traced it to the 1960s. In case you haven't heard it, the story goes that a female is driving alone on a highway when a car begins following her closely and menacingly. She panics and begins driving faster and faster—not realizing that the driver behind her is trying to warn her that a man with a knife is in her backseat.

1998's *Urban Legend* opens with a dramatized version of this urban legend, though it had been a part of slumber party and campfire stories for years before that. Whether or not the legend is based on any fact is debatable. But one thing is for sure—it's hard to get sneaked up on in a two-seater car, so consider trading that reliable sedan for a sporty little number that no murderer could dream of fitting into.

You might want to consider a more environmentally conscious and backseat-killer-proof moped.

SURVIVAL TIP

BE NICE—BUT NOT TOO NICE

IS THIS BECAUSE I DIDN'T INVITE YOU TO MY HOUSEWARMING?

This survival method is rich with irony. One way to avoid the wrath of a murderer? Be nice.

Everyone needs a friend. Someone to bitch to after a hard day's work. Someone to help you move. Someone to come over early when you're hosting a party so you're not the only person there when guests begin to arrive. But it's a fine line you walk here. Because if you've watched any horror movies, you know that if you're the killer's only friend, when she cracks, you're gonna get it. And you're gonna get it bad.

Now, you can't go the exact opposite route here either—anyone who purposefully excludes or God forbid bullies a psycho is bound to get killed. So what do you do if you find yourself in the same office, school, apartment building, or neighborhood as someone who screams "Potential Serial Killer"? Only one word can save you here: *acquaintance.*

That's right. You want to acquaint yourself with the potentially murderous psycho. Yet you have to avoid getting too close and ultimately disappointing her, thus resulting in your certain and bloody demise. And you really don't want to isolate her to the point where once she snaps, she is likely to set into motion your certain and bloody demise.

How do you go about affirming your role as Official Acquaintance of Murderous Psychos? I present to you the Scream Queen's Dos and Don'ts for Making Acquaintances:

Do:
- Volunteer to get the mail for your killer acquaintance when she is out of town.

Don't:
- Accept any invitations to accompany her on her vacation.

Do:
- Send a card when the mother of the suspected murderer dies, even though he probably killed her.

Don't:
- Bring over a casserole when the mother of the suspected murderer dies and then agree to stay and eat it with him.

Do:
- Let moving trucks park in front of your house when the new neighbor you suspect of being a killer is moving in next door.

Don't:
- Let the new neighbor you suspect may crack and kill someone use any of your storage space to stash some

spare boxes after he moves in next door. Hint: there are bloody weapons in those boxes and he just wants to frame you for the murder of his entire family, whom he buried in the backyard of his old house.

Presumably, you can keep your shit together enough to avoid becoming a mortal enemy of a murderous psycho. But the line between "acquaintance" and "friend" is a bit blurry, and it's one worth paying attention to. Stay close, but not too close, lest you want your new buddy to dye her hair to match yours, bang your man, kill your puppy, and ultimately stab your boyfriend to death with her own stiletto. Not that you could blame her—she was just looking out for you.

 SCREAM QUEEN SAYS *I don't think I have to tell you that these rules extend to Facebook. "Yes, I'll accept your Friendship. No, I won't comment when you post new pictures on your wall."*

SKIP PROM

HERE'S TO A NIGHT TO REMEMBER . . .

Ah, prom. The dresses. The dates. The dancing.

The bodies. The blood. The bludgeoning.

For some people (mostly girls whose highest aspirations include being voted Best Looking in their high school yearbook), prom is the greatest night of their lives. Getting dressed up, having fun with friends and a cute guy, and taking a limo to a fancy banquet hall (or a sweaty high school gym) to steal sips of cheap vodka and dance is the perfect way to commemorate the end of high school. Unless, of course, you're in a horror movie. In that case, prom is a good way to get yourself killed in a particularly nasty, very unglamorous way.

We've already covered the story of the most notorious prom-goer, Carrie, whose evening didn't exactly go as planned. But the long and treasured history of cinematic prom-night horror doesn't end with pig's blood and John Travolta.

⚠ In both the 1980 and 2008 versions of *Prom Night*, a vengeful and uninvited prom guest is dead set on ruining the night for a group of friends. In the slasher '80s version, prom night falls on the anniversary of the accidental death of a young girl named Robin who fell to her death when a group of girls backed her into a corner while teasing her. That same group of girls, now high school seniors (including the mother of all Scream Queens, Jamie Lee Curtis), are getting ready for a memorable evening, despite the news that the man falsely charged with Robin's death has escaped from prison. As you might guess, it's a recipe for disaster and let's just say that not many prom goers made it to the after-party. But equally unsurprising, the Scream Queen Jamie Lee remains standing, axe in hand.

In the 2008, less slasher, more crappy version of *Prom Night*, the night is marred by the recent parole of a man convicted of stalking one of his young students, now (you guessed it!) a high school senior attending the prom with a group of friends. One by one, the seniors commit egregious horror movie errors—from sex to boozing to hiding under the bed. And not surprisingly, each pays dearly, except of course for the Scream Queen (this time played by a very non-badass Brittany Snow) who manages to escape her vengeful stalker's pathetic attempts to get back at her for his "unwarranted" imprisonment. ⚠

Prom night is a nightmare on many levels. In life, it's a haze of reminiscing, vomit, and drunken tears. In horror movies, as you've seen, it quickly goes from being "the best night of your life" to "the last night of your life." So when that late spring evening rolls around and you find yourself caught up in the promises of taffeta and slow dances, think about staying home. Or better yet, get as far away from the prom as possible. You can check out the pictures on Facebook, and sleep soundly knowing that you won't be climbing the stairway to heaven.

 SCREAM QUEEN SAYS *A wrist corsage isn't much of a weapon.*

WHAT'S IN A NAME? APPARENTLY A RECIPE FOR HORROR

Open Water is based on the true story of vacationers Tim and Eileen Lonergan, who in 1998 were left to perish off the Great Barrier Reef after a charter SCUBA company stranded the two.

In the film version of their real-life horror story, the characters are named Daniel Kintner and Susan Watkins. So what, right? Well, the inspiration for these characters names are Alex Kintner and Chrissie Watkins, two of the shark-attack victims in *Jaws*.

Seems like the makers of *Open Water* were trying to see if anyone was paying attention. But it doesn't take a hardcore movie fan (or a detective) to know that things wouldn't end well for Daniel and Susan. The sharks show up pretty much right after the boat takes off.

Sharks may not be the most common killer in horror movies, but those friggin' teeth sure can ruin a beach day.

DON'T TELL YOUR FRIENDS YOU'LL BE RIGHT BACK

I'LL BE RIGHT BACK? OH NO YOU DIDN'T . . .

Our everyday vocabulary is full of phrases that we use when we mean the exact opposite. Take, for example:

WHEN WE SAY	WE REALLY MEAN
Let's just be friends.	Let's just never talk again.
Fine, thanks. How are you?	You're too insignificant to me for me to take the time to tell you that I am melancholy at best.
Dry clean only.	Dry clean only. But the people who made this shirt know you're just going to throw it in the washing machine with the rest of your normal clothes.
It's not you, it's me.	It's definitely you. There's nothing wrong with me.

And, in horror movies, the mother of all empty phrases:

WHEN THEY SAY	IT REALLY MEANS
I'll be right back.	You're never going to see me again. It's only a matter of minutes until someone brutally murders me. Buh-bye!

In dozens of horror films through the decades, "I'll be right back" let the audience know a character was doomed. This survival tip should come as no surprise. After all, it ties into several others. "I'll be right back" is often murmured before someone goes to check out the fuse box, goes for help, or breaks off from the group. It's a prelude to a kiss of death.

You don't hear the ol' "I'll be right back" in recent horror movies because it was so overused for so long that it's now somewhat of a joke. But for a long time, what followed those four little words was far from funny.

 **SCREAM QUEEN SAYS** *"I'm about to killed"* would be more direct.

SPEND THOSE TEENAGE YEARS SOMEPLACE SAFE

ONLY THE GOOD DIE YOUNG? IN HORROR FLICKS, ONLY THE STUPID DIE TEEN.

For the average American, the teenage years are the worst. Bad skin. Broken hearts. Long limbs and flat chests. A weird place between childhood and adulthood, the teen years are often the time when no one is sure where she wants to be, but she knows it's not where she is. Teenage angst is angst at its most traumatic and poetic. In horror movies, the teenage years are downright horrific.

Perhaps it's because teenagers like nothing more than drinking, swearing, and doing the nasty. Maybe it's because they're such insensitive assholes that they tease and harass anyone they deem inferior to themselves, which is pretty much everyone, making them a target for revenge. Or maybe it's just because teenage girls and guys look the best when they're running.

Popular horror movies have gone through different phases over the years—from slasher flicks to psycho thrillers to sarcastic, tongue-in-cheek horror comedies, to bad remakes of classics. But one vein of the horror genre that's never going away is the teenage horror movie. Here are just a few movies in which most of the victims were pimply, horny, and too young to drink legally:

- *The Faculty*
- *Urban Legend*
- *Halloween I*, *II*, and *IV*, and *Halloween H20*
- the *Scream* triology
- *I Know What You Did Last Summer*
- *Final Destination I* and *II*
- *Carrie*
- *Ginger Snaps*
- *Prom Night*
- *The Slumber Party Massacre*
- *A Nightmare on Elm Street* series

You can't avoid your teenage years. Eventually, all twelve-year-olds turn thirteen and after that, they face seven years that are rich with potential for horror. All you can do is watch your step. During those exceptionally dangerous teen years, pay even more attention to the Scream Queen's survival tips. Your teenage years are bound to be horrible. But if you make your decisions wisely, the only trauma you suffer may be of the standard "your best friend sleeps with your boyfriend" variety.

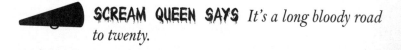 **SCREAM QUEEN SAYS** *It's a long bloody road to twenty.*

PLAY NICE

PLAY NICE AND YOU GET TO KEEP ALL YOUR FINGERS!

This one's a toughie. In situations where you are being stalked by a murderer, things tend to get stressful and leave tensions high. In many horror movies, this is exaggerated by the fact that a group of people are often locked up or otherwise stuck together in situations that leave them prone to bickering. But in some ways, horror movies are a lot like Little League baseball teams. No matter the situation, it's best to stick together and play nice. Once the team members begin to fight amongst themselves, they play like shit, and no one wins. This logic extends off the field, too. In a horror movie-esque situation, even when the axe is about to drop, don't let the intensity get to you. Because in a horror movie, once people start to pick at each other, those same people start to get picked off.

Maybe killers' dislike for fights stems from an unpleasant home life during childhood. Most murderers grew up in less than ideal situations, and arguing mothers and fathers top the list of Reasons to Become a Murderous Psycho. Alternatively, it could be a dislike for loud noises (although they've picked a strange profession if they dislike screaming). Whatever the reason, the proof is undeniable. Check out just some of the movies where fighting contributed to a group's demise:

- *The Blair Witch Project*: once the lost campers started to bicker amongst themselves, things went downhill pretty fast.
- *I Know What You Did Last Summer*: start to finish, this annoying group of whiny and unrealistically hot friends are at each other's throats—they were doomed from the start.

- *The Mist*: not just a regular fight, but a religious fight over whether or not these citizens caught in the grocery store are being punished by God, this captive crew bickers and debates until there's almost no one left—you'd think they could have thought of more productive ways to spend their last few hours.

If you find yourself stuck with a group of people, hiding out from or held captive by someone who is playing with a deck that's short a few cards, keep your nice face on. Let the other idiots throw the insults and the punches—they can be the ones whose limbs start flying.

 SCREAM QUEEN SAYS *What's the matter? Never earned "Plays well with others" on your report card?*

SURVIVAL TIP

DON'T TAKE A VACATION TO REPAIR YOUR RELATIONSHIP

AFTER A FEW HOURS IN THE SUN, ALL OUR PROBLEMS WILL BE SOLVED!

The vacation or long weekend has often been used as a half-assed attempt to save a relationship. On the verge of separate beds and possibly separate bank accounts, couples optimistically and unrealistically think that three to seven days in a warm climate will give them a clean slate and they'll return home with a tan and renewed commitment to their relationship. Dumbasses.

It's ridiculous to think for one flippin' second that this lame attempt at rekindling a relationship would work any better in a horror movie than in real life. In fact, as you may have already guessed, it actually goes a hell of a lot worse.

In both the 1978 and 2008 versions of *Long Weekend,* a couple who openly despises each other take off for a (you guessed it!) long weekend with the goal of reconnecting (when they're not psychologically torturing each other). In the earlier and undeniably better version, the couple goes camping so they can use the expensive hiking equipment the husband recently bought, much to the chagrin of his nightmarish wife. In the 2008 version, the couple's vacation is beachier but the premise is the same—they hope all of their problems will go away once they've changed the backdrop for their horrible and loveless relationship. Let's just say that after the long weekend, their relationship was no longer their biggest concern.

In 1984's *Children of the Corn,* a young couple heads out on a road trip (mistake numero uno) to California. As if being forced to ride a long distance in a car with someone you've grown to despise wasn't bad enough, they hit the body of an already-deceased child. Their attempt to report the crime leads them to a not-so-friendly town where once again, their relationship problems are put on the back burner by the psychotic residents of the village.

If your relationship is dying a slow death, don't try to delay the inevitable or simply switch locations, thinking all your problems will go away. As these movies have taught us, things will only get worse—for both of you—if you take your misery show on the road. Pull your dying relationship off life support in the comforts of your home—no passport required.

 SCREAM QUEEN SAYS *You don't have to worry about packing the perfect outfit to break up in, either.*

BE A GOOD GIRL—THE PUNISHMENT ISN'T WORTH IT

THE PUNISHMENT WILL FIT THE CRIME . . . AND THEN SOME.

Life as a goody-two-shoes can be mundane. You've already learned that if you want to keep your head, you can't drink, do drugs, swear, have sex, or fight. Staying alive can sometimes require living a boring existence. So what happens when that call of the wild is too hard to resist? After all, if you wanted to live like a nun, you would have enrolled at a convent. But, if you do decide to break the rules, you better hope you don't get caught. Once you're deemed a troublemaker, you're bound to attract trouble. And if that trouble is in a horror movie, you know it's going to end with a battle.

One particular Japanese horror film, 2000's *Batoru Rowairu* (translation: *Battle Royale*), centers around a group of high school freshmen whose disillusionment with their lives and bleak futures manifests in bad behavior. Seeking payback for their troublemaking, a teacher forces them to take part in a government experiment, Battle Royale.

After being misled and drugged into submission, the entire class is brought to an isolated island. There, they are fitted with collars that have been programmed to detonate in thirty-six hours—unless the students complete the assigned mission of killing each other off until only one is left standing. The students handle the battle differently—some are determined not to play the game and try to hide, whereas others adapt quickly and embrace the game in order to increase their chances of survival. It's a twisted, bloody mess that speaks volumes about what humans will resort to when their survival depends on it. Try to figure out any scenario in which this movie could possible have a happy ending.

This is a hidden gem of a horror flick (with an American version reportedly in the works) that any Scream Queen should see . . . especially if you are feeling inclined to be a little delinquent yourself. The next time you feel limited by the rules of horror survival, consider the punishment that may be waiting for you should you choose to misbehave. You never know who's going to have your back if you find yourself on your own little class trip.

 SCREAM QUEEN SAYS *When you misbehave in a horror movie, you're usually looking at a punishment way worse than grounding.*

BEWARE TEENAGE DISENCHANTMENT
PRETTY SOON, I'LL DITCH THIS PODUNK TOWN AND NEVER LOOK BACK!

As if things weren't sucky enough for teenagers who have grown bored in the limbo between childhood and adulthood, someone has to come along and kill them. Often brutally. In a manner that earns an R-rating.

Many teenagers who fall into the 87 percent of the population who don't enjoy playing varsity sports, having really bad sex, and hanging out at the Gas-N-Sip get through their teen years relatively unscathed. They comfort themselves by listening to a lot of Paramore and puffing on (but not inhaling) more than their fair share of American Spirits. They roll their eyes at their parents and discuss their superiority over the entire population of their high school to their one to three close friends. After graduation, no one in their hometown ever thinks of them again—until they inevitably become 1) good-looking, or 2) rich, and their Facebook friends start stalking them. All in all, they live pretty typical lives.

Then there are the disenchanted teens of horror movies. The Carries. The Sidney Prescotts. The Needys. Never quite satisfied with their adolescent existence, their every move expresses their desire to get far, far from away from the town they live in and most of the people they know. That's where the trouble starts.

You'd think that serial killers, not high up on the popularity pyramid themselves, would be sympathetic to people who disliked their teen years as much as the killers themselves most likely did. But no. Quite the opposite, in fact. If we can learn from horror movies (and you know we can), these knife-loving freaks are bound and determined to make their victims' teenage years even more unpleasant.

The secret for living out your teenage years is simple. Keep the gauge on your teenage angst meter pointing somewhere in the middle. Sure, you can roll your eyes at your parents and yell, "You just don't understand!" when they won't let you go to Aberdeen, Washington to weep over Kurt Cobain's grave. But keep that Cure T-shirt in your drawer and try not to plot the downfall of anyone much more popular than yourself. Believe me, they'll get theirs.

 SCREAM QUEEN SAYS *If you have Sylvia Plath poetry written on the knees of your jeans, you may as well kiss those legs goodbye.*

DON'T BE THE ONE TO GO FOR HELP

YOU GUYS STAY HERE ... I'LL GO FOR HELP.

You have to admire The One Who Goes for Help in horror movies. He has everyone's best interests at heart; he's willing to risk his own safety for that of the larger group. Don't get attached to him, though. Guaranteed—he's going to get wiped out, big time.

Think back to every slasher flick you've ever seen. Has it ever ended well for the person who offers to take one for the team? Take Stephen King's *The Mist*. After a mysterious fog of unknown origins invades a small town, a group of twenty or so people find themselves held captive in the grocery store, unable to venture outside as the mist—or whoever is in it—has started knocking people off left and right.

⚠ Nervous that they're running the risk of losing electricity (there's that whole "checkin' the fuse box" thing again), a young stock boy offers to go outside and fix the generator. His payback for being so generous? A giant tentacle appears out of the mist, grabs him, and begins to rip him to shreds. So much for checking that generator. ⚠

Later, when a larger group decides to venture out for help, they're met with a similar fate. Putting his trust in a standard weight rope (WTF?), the first of the group heads out into the mist, with who else but the guy from *Hung* holding on to the end of the rope. Surprise, surprise—turns out a giant monster with tentacles is stronger than a rope can handle. The man does make it back to the grocery store, but unfortunately, it's in two pieces. So much for being helpful.

The trend of killing the one who goes for help isn't limited to this movie, but I think you get what I mean here. Your best bet when you're hiding out from someone or something? Fly below the radar. Don't go vying for the role of top dog, don't try reverse psychology and mock a murderer into sparing you, and, as we've seen here, definitely don't try to be the boy scout. Stay put and hope that if you are stuck somewhere when a monster is coming after you, you have someone a bit more hardcore than a grocery store clerk looking out for you.

 SCREAM QUEEN SAYS *Clean up in aisle five.*

COUNT TO TEN BEFORE THAT MERCY KILL
FILE THIS UNDER INFORMATION THAT WOULD HAVE BEEN HANDY YESTERDAY!

No one likes a quitter—not even murderers. Perhaps that's why every time someone in a horror movie decides to Kevorkian herself or someone else to spare a more brutal ending, help arrives right after she pulls the trigger.

 In 2004's *Open Water*, a married couple, Daniel and Susan, find themselves stranded in the middle of the ocean after being accidentally left behind while scuba diving on an Australian vacation. Because no one realizes that the couple has been left behind until the next morning, sharks make mincemeat out of Daniel before the search team even goes looking for him. Left alone and soon to be shark bait herself, Susan finally decides to take her own life by removing her mask and drowning herself. Here comes the happy ending. Right after Susan gives in to the sharks, that less-than-reliable rescue team comes-a-lookin' for her. Bummer. While not exactly a horror movie, I can think of nothing scarier than looking on as your husband becomes shark food and knowing the same fate is not far in your future. What's even more terrifying is that this mediocre thriller was based on a true story. Jumping jellyfish, Batman— that sucks.

In *The Mist*, the aforementioned grocery store horror flick, hope begins to wear thin as the mist wipes out more and more people. Finally, David escapes the grocery store with his young son and three other survivors and they take off in an SUV, determined to find their way out of the mist. After encountering both David's wife's body and a huge, six-tentacle monster, the SUV runs out of gas and they are left with no options—other than killing themselves. Armed with a gun that contains only four bullets, Brave Dave says he will be the one who stays behind to be ripped apart by the beast, and shoots his four companions, including his own son. Climbing out of the SUV, David urges the monster to come and get him—but to no avail. The monster will not be provoked. Instead, help finally arrives, only moments after David kills the others. Hey, would you expect a feel-good ending from Stephen King? ⚠

So if you are ever tempted to pursue an active role in your own demise, take a breather and count to ten. If horror movies have shown us anything, help is right around the corner.

SCREAM QUEEN SAYS *Give that trigger finger a scratch.*

SURVIVAL TIP

DITCH THE GIRL WHO CAN'T STOP CRYING

CRYING IT OUT MAY HELP YOU FEEL BETTER . . . BUT TRUST ME, THE RELIEF IS SHORT-LIVED.

There's no way to not sound like a cold-hearted biotch here. When someone with murderous intentions is pursuing you, keep your shit together. The weepy chick is never highly regarded by the killer. Even if she lives, she's most likely brought back in a sequel to be tormented even further. So avoid being That Girl, and, if you're in the company of that girl, watch out. She may as well have a target on her back.

At the risk of sounding cliché (irony: noted!), crying never got anyone anywhere. Neither did any of these emotional freak-outs often uttered in horror movies:

- "Why are you doing this to me?!" Honestly, did these girls expect an answer besides, "Because I f***ing feel like it?" Mass murderers are not known for their reasoning.
- "Please . . . I'll do anything." Two words here: d-uh. You mean you have an alternative to watching your own blood gush from your body? What a clever gal you must be.
- "What's the matter with you?" Listen, this is no time to share feelings. You can't deny the fact that killers are *go get 'em!* kinds of guys. If he wanted to unburden his soul, he would have. Instead, he'll unburden someone of her bowels, mmmkay?
- "Stop." Oh, okay. Silly me. I thought you were enjoying me ripping you limb from limb. I must have misread you.

The Crying Chick appears in every horror movie. Let's take a look some of the most notable criers in all of horror whose fates ranged from Scream Queen Solid to Dead as a Doornail. In no particular order . . .

- Drew Barrymore, *Scream*. It's amazing she could eke out a cry at all, what with the weird way she talks out of the side of her mouth all the time.
- Shelley Duvall, *The Shining*. Is it me, or did poor Shelley look a bit ridiculous throughout this entire movie? Maybe it was the weird Laura Ingalls Wilder dress she wore. Maybe it was the fact that Jack Nicholson probably made, like, ten zillion times more money on that movie than she did. Either way, her crying was irritating and

grating. Instead of feeling badly for her, I mostly got annoyed.

- Neve Campbell, *Scream* trilogy. Every scene that Campbell cried in over the course of these movies looks like it was just lifted from *Party of Five*. You remember *Party of Five*, don't you? It was that other show in which Neve Campbell cried a lot.

- Paris Hilton, *House of Wax*. She cried harder when she was sent to jail for forty-five days in 2007. Don't get me wrong—prison doesn't sound like any fun. But getting impaled by a huge metal pole would probably be scarier than a short stint in Heiress Jail.

- Jamie Lee Curtis. Jamie Lee Curtis has actually called her talent for realistic crying one of her best assets as an actress. She sure did get a lot of practice in *Prom Night*, *The Fog*, *Terror Train*, *Roadgames*, *Halloween*, *Halloween II*, *Halloween III*, *Halloween H20*, *Halloween Resurrection*, and *My Girl*. What, like you didn't cry when the Macaulay Culkin character died?

- Sissy Spacek, *Carrie*. Between the shower scene, her freaky mother, brutal classmates, and the bucket of pig blood, perhaps Sissy was the most justified in her tears.

It's hard not to shed a tear when someone is intent on removing your limbs. If you find yourself in a particularly tear-inducing situation, go to that happy place in your head. Remember that your fear is temporary. The bad crap will be out of the way in no time . . . in one way or another.

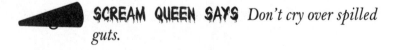 **SCREAM QUEEN SAYS** *Don't cry over spilled guts.*

HORROR WHERE YOU LEAST EXPECT IT: BIG LOVE

You expect to see some scary stuff on a television drama about modern-day Mormon fundamentalists living a polygamist lifestyle in Utah—especially when the show is on HBO, home of full-frontal male nudity and the creepily brilliant *Six Feet Under* (now six feet under itself). But viewers got something way scarier than the threat of a foursome with Bill Paxton, who provided the only external genitalia in the show's fourth season.

Thinking she was just retrieving bacon from her mother's walk-in freezer, Nikki (played by fashionista Chloe Sevigny, who must be terrified every time she has to throw on an ankle-length dress and buttoned-to-the-neck floral blouse) discovers the frozen body of her father, Roman Grant, who was forced to chill out after an angry Mormon smothered him with a pillow. The actor who played Grant, Harry Dean Stanton (whom we loved in *Pretty in Pink*), is scary enough when he's walking around and talking. Drain the color from his face and stick him in a freezer? That's tinkle-your-pants scary. Almost as scary as those Mormon bangs.

SURVIVAL TIP
DON'T CHEAT ON YOUR BOYFRIEND
IN HORROR MOVIES, SEX IS NEVER SAFE.

They say you only hurt the one you love. Well, in horror movies, everyone gets hurt. And there's a whole lot of naughty sex going on. So I guess the saying is true here.

Horror movie or not, cheating never goes well. Sure, every once in a while someone gets away with it. But 99 percent of the time, you get caught—sometimes involving a painful and burning rash somewhere south of your belly button that you've so generously passed on to your boyfriend. But if you're in a horror movie and you get caught cheating, herpes will be the best part of your day.

In the 1990 movie *Buried Alive*, a woman named Joanna cheats on her husband with a wealthy doctor. In an effort to spend the rest of their lives together, Joanna and the doctor, Cort, hatch a plan to kill her husband, Clint, and enjoy his insurance money. Apparently, this Cort guy isn't the best of doctors, however. Their attempt to kill Clint by giving him an overdose of drugs fails—and Clint wakes up to find himself . . . (wait for it) buried alive. As you might guess, Clint isn't too thrilled about Joanna and Cort. Needless to say, they don't get to enjoy that insurance money.

Unfortunately, the "don't cheat" rule in horror movies isn't limited to husbands and wives. In *May*, the title character has a brief relationship with a lesbian she works with. Even though it was pretty clear to everyone but May that this woman, the way-hotter Polly (played by Anna Faris) wasn't too serious about their fling, this comes as a surprise to May—and she does not handle the surprise well.

It's a real bitch to survive a horror movie—and the no-cheating rule is sure to take the wind out of a few slutty sails. What can I say? Have you ever had a roll in the hay that was worth getting your throat slashed?

 **SCREAM QUEEN SAYS** *That would have to be some hay.*

CHAPTER 8

THE WEIRD KID IN YOUR GYM CLASS

In high school, people fall into two camps: the beautiful crowd and everyone else. And within that "everyone else" group there are freaks, weirdos, loners, geeks, nerds, and dorks. If they're lucky, the beautiful kids regard them as furniture, a backdrop to the best four years of their beautiful lives. But in a lot of cases, these rejects are not so lucky and the beautiful people do everything in their power to torture those who are lower in the high school hierarchy. Sometimes, these tortured kids manage to look forward to bigger and better things. They regard those four years as a stepping stone to the rest of their lives, in which they'll never have to see their beautiful harassers ever again. Other times though, the tormented kids don't have the perspective necessary to brush it off. And if these kids are in a horror movie, well, things get a bit . . . messy.

BE NICER THAN NECESSARY TO LONERS

PAYBACK IS A BITCH, ESPECIALLY IN A HORROR MOVIE . . .

We've already established the fact that most serial killers suffer from some form of Daddy Never Hugged Me Syndrome. And odds are, they weren't captains of anything besides the Hey! Pick on Me Team. So when they reach the age of revenge and slashing, who do you think their first targets will be? Hint: every person who ever bullied or played a prank on them.

True, sometimes, loners are loners for a reason. Maybe they have a kind of weird smell or talk about things no one else cares about, like their feelings or thoughts. Or maybe they themselves aren't particularly offensive, but they have a strict family who makes them join the Mathletes or Comp Sci club. You most likely don't *want* to befriend a loner—and you don't have to (not really—see *Play Nice* in Chapter 7). However, if horror movies have taught us one thing about these finicky little freaks, it's this: you sure don't want to be mean to them.

We've seen people exacting revenge on their bullies in many horror movies. But the most brutal has to be 2010's *The Final*. This dark and twisted film follows a group of high school students whose school days are a fun mix of isolation, humiliation, ridicule, and emotional and physical abuse. Tired of the torture they encounter when they're just trying to get through the day, these rejects, led by a likable loser, Dane, plan their revenge on the popular kids at their school in a big way. Making use of a large and luxurious lake house that Dane's uncle willed to him when he died, the group throws a costume party at the house—without ever revealing who the hosts are. Drawing inspiration from their classes and from their favorite movies, the losers drug all the guests so they are sleepy and vulnerable . . . and then wake them up to show them their favorite tricks from their favorite film genre—romantic comedies! Just kidding. These kids are horror freaks and they use some of the freakiest shit out there to pay back the douchiest of the douches for the years of torture.

Who's left out of this scary-ass costume ball? Those who didn't go out of their way to ruin the lives of these poor kids. What a novel idea! This is one survival tip you should have no trouble following: don't harass anyone and you'll be left out of their emotionally charged revenge plots. If you choose to ignore this one, what can I say? You get what you deserve.

 SCREAM QUEEN SAYS *The payback makes a wedgie look like a day in the park.*

SURVIVAL TIP

DISCOURAGE THE ONE WITH THE PIG BLOOD

YA KNOW, MAN, I HAVE A BAD FEELING ABOUT THIS . . .

When it comes to horror movies, it's safe to say there is always a fair bit of collateral damage. The hotel in *The Shining* probably had to undergo a serious renovation to fix all those axe marks and slashes in the doors and furniture. And you can figure that whenever someone uses a chainsaw indoors, he's going to slip a few times with the blade and leave some gouges that call for a repair job. ⚠️ In *Scream*, we saw a pretty-badass-for-the-'90s TV destroyed when Sidney finally kills Stu. ⚠️ But in some movies, the collateral damage is a bit harder to replace. We're talking about actual people who meet their demises when the shit hits the fan.

Everyone knows that in the horror classic, 1976's *Carrie*, based on the novel of the same title by Stephen King, an entire senior class is wiped out due to the mean antics of a small group of assholes, including a pre-Scientology John Travolta. The only one who survives is Sue, a girl who is nice enough to offer up the services of her boyfriend to take Carrie to the prom where the big scene goes down—pig blood, telekinetically set fire, and all. Sue actually tried to stop the douchebags from humiliating Carrie. Too bad it was just a bit too late. Carrie is humiliated, exacts punishment on everyone who was unlucky enough to be at the prom, and it's lights out from there. Even poor Sue ended up with a ragin' case of PTSD.

If you find yourself in a horrific situation, try being one step ahead of the too-late Sue. If you can't actually convince some jackass to put down the proverbial pig blood, then stay the hell away from him, her, or them. That way, you won't end up as living, breathing (er, dying, gasping) collateral damage.

 SCREAM QUEEN SAYS *You probably don't know someone with telekinesis—but why take the chance?*

SEND YOUR REGRETS TO THE PARTY THAT'S HELD IN THE MIDST OF A MURDERER'S RAMPAGE

THERE'S A SERIAL KILLER ON THE LOOSE AND HE'S TARGETING TEENS. ARE YOU THINKING WHAT I'M THINKING? PARTY!

You gotta give teenagers in horror movies credit—they are nothing if not determined. Escaped mental patient? Those kids will still have the prom. News of a bad storm threatening to cut out power for much of the area? They're still going to their parents' cabin in the mountains! Town being terrorized by a string of murders? BFD. Those kids are still gonna rip it up.

In a way, it's a nice courtesy on the part of the partygoers. Serial killing can be a draining profession. There's the stalking, the plotting, the hacking—and the cleanup is a real bitch! Why not make the killer's job a tiny bit easier and gather in a large group so he has his choice of victims? But if you're not trying to give the slasher his pick of the litter, do yourself a favor and do not attend any parties until safety has been restored.

In 1982's *The Slumber Party Massacre*, new girl Valerie has the good sense to skip the sleepover that her neighbor is hosting in light of her parents' trip out of town. True, her reasons for not attending have more to do with mean girls' petty high school bullshit than the threat of a recent prison escapee crashing the party with his two-foot power drill, but either way she dodges a bullet.  In fact, she actually manages to take the murderer down. In your face, mean girls.

If your town is under attack by a psychotic killer with a taste for blood or is conveniently located one exit away from a mental institution, head someplace safer than a house party filled with obnoxious, drunk teenagers that anyone—even someone who's most violent action to date has been slapping away a mosquito—might consider killing, especially if they play one more freakin' Lady Gaga song.

SCREAM QUEEN SAYS *Murder on the dance floor!*

IF A POTENTIAL LOVE INTEREST IS ALREADY DATING AN OBJECT, LEAVE THEM TO THEIR HAPPINESS

DO YOU HAVE A GIRLFRIEND? PERHAPS A LARGE MANNEQUIN YOU'RE INVOLVED WITH?

Hey, everyone has her own tastes. Some girls love juiceheads with arms like tree trunks and abs you could wash your clothes on, while others go for the scrawny emo-types with haircuts more commonly seen on toddlers. Some guys like the naughty librarian type while others go for huge boobs and small brains. And some people . . . well, some people prefer the company of an inanimate object.

In 2002's *May*, a young girl, unable to make real friends because of a lazy eye and a corrective eye patch, befriends a large china doll that her mother gives to her. She plays with the doll and talks to her; the doll soon becomes her best friend. That's all well and good while May is a young girl. Not so good when May becomes an adult and continues her twisted relationship with the doll.

Despite a pallor generally found only on those dorks from *Twilight*, May eventually finds herself a boyfriend. But, not surprisingly, she isn't capable of maintaining a healthy relationship with a man considering her only social connection in the twenty years prior has been with an object who can't talk or move. Unfortunately for the poor guy she decides is her soul mate, May goes nuts and kills him (as well as a coworker with whom May has a brief lesbian encounter). Don't worry, there's a lot more to this freaky little picture and I didn't give away the ending here. Besides, if you couldn't imagine that the woman who is friends with a doll goes nuts and kills some people, well, you haven't learned anything yet.

In 1978's *Magic*, a young woman named Peg considers leaving her husband for her high school sweetheart, Corky, when he returns to their hometown. The only problem is, Corky's best friend Fats is a bit jealous. "Fats" is kind of a funny name for a guy, don't you think? Well, not for a ventriloquist dummy—which is exactly what Fats is. Peg manages to dodge a bullet, but not before Corky and Fats wreak some havoc in the small town.

It's hard to resist primal urges. If you become interested in someone who already has a significant other from the Inanimate Objects Family, try your best to squash those feelings. Even if you don't end up killed, you'll eventually find yourself in a threesome ripe with potential for getting a splinter in a really bad spot.

 SCREAM QUEEN SAYS *Be a doll and be nice to the kid who's in love with an object.*

SURVIVAL TIP

BEWARE OF ANY BOY WHO LIKES MOMMY A LITTLE BIT TOO MUCH

A BOY'S BEST FRIEND IS HIS MOTHER . . .

Every guy you'll ever date will have mommy issues. He will constantly seek her approval. Or he will resent her for babying him. Whatever the issue, it will affect your relationship—it's up to you to decide how much you let it. But in horror movies, mommy issues play out a little bit differently . . . they can make both you and your guy *Psycho*.

Alfred Hitchcock's *Psycho* is, of course, the mother of all mommy-issue horror movies. If you haven't already seen this movie, you should be ashamed of yourself. But if you have, you know the image that sticks in your mind even more than Marion being hacked to bits is ⚠ Norman dressed up as his dead mother—the mother who is actually decomposing in the basement of the house next to the Bates Motel. ⚠ But Hitchcock isn't the only horror director to make use of these mommy issues so familiar to psychos and psychiatrists alike.

In life, you'll rarely get such a straightforward indication that something might be up with your mommy-centric boyfriend as you might in a horror movie. And because mommy-issues can be indicative of homicidal issues, you should be aware of any funny stuff going on between your man and the woman who gave him life. To help you decide when things are getting a bit too cozy between your guy and his mom, here's The Scream Queen's Guide to Sniffing Out Momma's Boys.

You know your boyfriend is too into his mom if:

- He takes you home after a night of drinking and, instead of some heavy petting, you're treated to milk and cookies with his mom . . . who has been waiting up for him (even though he's twenty-four).
- Your first date consists of picking up his mother after her colonoscopy and watching daytime episodes of *Who Wants to Be a Millionaire?* with her until the sedation wears off.
- For your birthday, he treats you to a facial and mani-pedi at the spa. Carpooling is easy because he and his mom have a couple massage booked for the same time.
- He has a picture of his prom night on his bedside table— and his date was his mother.
- Every year on his birthday, he celebrates by watching a video of his birth.

I don't mean to cause alarm. After all, not all guys with mommy issues become murderous psychopaths. But wouldn't you rather know what you were getting into before you find yourself forced to choose between playing Mommy and Naughty Son and being stabbed to death in the shower?

 SCREAM QUEEN SAYS *If you meet a guy with two dads, grab him. Not only is mom not an issue, he's more likely to be a sharp dresser.*

SURVIVAL TIP

IF YOU'VE ALWAYS BEEN A LOSER, QUESTION THE PERSON WHO ALL OF A SUDDEN WANTS TO DATE YOU

I'VE ALWAYS WANTED TO ASK YOU OUT. I WAS JUST INTIMIDATED BY THE GROUP OF FRIENDS THAT WAS NEVER SURROUNDING YOU.

Everyone has gone through a dry spell once or twice in her life—times when it seemed you couldn't buy a date. But then there are girls whose lives are one looong dry spell. These girls have come to terms with the fact that, as much of a bummer as it is, they're probably going to end up alone. Hey, they can always get cats.

In horror movies, we see lots of these types. Socially awkward loners who don't stand a chance of finding someone to hang out with. But all is not lost. Every once in a while, just when this poor loser is convinced she's doomed to a solitary existence, someone who is willing to date her pops into her life. Despite the fact that this turn of events is as unprecedented as one of the Kardashian sisters offering insightful comments on the current socioeconomic state of America, the life-long loner is so happy to find companionship that she doesn't even question the guy's motive. She just accepts the new attention as pure affection, and everything goes downhill from there.

In *Carrie*, after seventeen years of isolation, the title character is asked out by one of the most popular guys in school after his girlfriend's guilty conscience drives her to offer his services as a prom date. True, Tommy is actually coming from a good place—but without him acting as her prom date, Carrie would have probably just stayed home and cried into her ice cream like any other loner on prom night. Instead, she goes to the prom with Tommy . . . and we all know how that turned out.

In *Jennifer's Body*, a socially irrelevant, emo type named Colin is thrilled when popular and beautiful Jennifer agrees to go on a date with him. Not for one second does he stop and wonder why someone as amazing as Jennifer would deign to hang out with someone as low on the totem pole as him. Poor kid . . . he actually seems surprised when she decides she would rather eat him than have sex with him.

It is possible to climb the social ladder in high school—but it's also highly unlikely. If every weekend of your young life has been spent crying while you post your newest poem to your blog, you might want to question the motives of the most popular guy in school if he all of a sudden can't live without you. He may actually just like you, especially if you've recently experienced growth in the chest region. But he could also be preparing to publicly humiliate you, offer you up for satanic sacrifice, or ingest your innards. So try not to get too flattered by the sudden attention—until you know if he's interested in dating you or eating you.

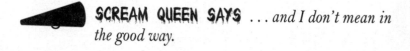 **SCREAM QUEEN SAYS** . . . *and I don't mean in the good way.*

PART 5

OH, FREAK OUT!

"YOU'RE A PERSISTENT LITTLE BASTARD,
AIN'T YA?"
—*CAMP BLOOD*

CHAPTER 9

UNDEAD AND IN DENIAL

No matter how much you prepare yourself, it's hard to accept death as an inevitable aspect of life. And, no, I'm not referring to the regular circle of life.

Rather, I'm talking about those pesky dead people who aren't too happy about their current status of not breathing. Zombies and other undead types are a persistent bunch—and they love eating the brains right out of pretty girls' heads. If you find yourself face-to-face with one, you'll need to be prepared for just how vengeful those rotting bastards can be. And when you're trying to kill someone who's already dead, things can get even trickier than usual.

God, can't a girl catch a break?!

DITCH YOUR HOBBIES

OOH, TAXIDERMY! NO BAD KARMA THERE.

Hobbies hold a lot of potential for bad stuff happening. Aside from the threat of bullying (*But guys, numismatics kicks ass! You don't know pure joy until you've been to the U.S. Mint!*) and the cost (*Only $450 for an original Sacajawean dollar!? Sold!*) involved with most hobbies, you have some potentially horrifying cons working against you.

First, many hobbies center around collecting old shit. And anytime there is old shit, there is the likely scenario that this shit once belonged to someone else. And if that someone is dead and didn't exactly volunteer to give you aforementioned shit, things can go bad rather quickly.

The dead are a finicky bunch. They don't care for people who step on their graves, they don't like it when people recognize their downfalls in less-than-sensitive fashions, and they don't like to be interrupted via Ouija board at high school sleepovers. But if you *really* want to piss them off, try messing with their stuff.

This makes as little sense to me as it does to you. They're dead! Why should they need anything, never mind their crappy old haunted journals? Unfortunately, it's not up to us and the dead are notoriously difficult to negotiate with. So if your hobby involves Old Shit That Used to Belong to Dead People, consider taking up something safer, like knitting. Although you do run the risk of getting stabbed with one of those needles . . .

Then there is the social isolation that seems to be close behind most hobbyists. As we've seen, horror movie loners tend to forge their way into the social world in a rather violent matter—like torturing the people who have been ignoring them for years or setting the whole gym on fire while the senior class just tries to enjoy their prom. So lest you run the risk of being the psycho who kills everyone and then ends up dead herself, here's a novel idea: why not try spending time with real people instead of stamps, coins, scrapbooks, quilts, and half-finished scarves? I know it may be painful to expand your social circle beyond the checkout lady at the craft store, but it could pay off in the long run.

There's also the potential for bad karmic energy surrounding your hobbies. Specifically, the karma surrounding one freaky-ass hobby that should go away. That's right, ladies, I'm asking the taxidermists among you to nix stuffing dead animals. I'm going to go out on a limb and guess that there aren't many of you, but I want to throw this out there anyway. Despite the creepiness factor of this nasty hobby, I can only think of one horror movie featuring a taxidermist, and it's a biggie: *Psycho*. True, things don't end particularly well for Norman, but spending the second half of your life in prison when the first half was spent living with/dressing up as your dead mother? Kind of a pathetic end to a pathetic beginning.

 SCREAM QUEEN SAYS *I'm sure there's a cool hobby out there that I'm missing, but damn if I can think of one.*

HORROR WHERE YOU LEAST EXPECT IT: CINDERELLA

When you think of wicked stepparents, your mind immediately goes to the wicked stepmother in the story of Cinderella. But that pointy-chinned witch from the Disney cartoon has nothing on the wicked stepmother that the Brothers Grimm wrote about in the original story.

In the original version, the stepmother was not only wicked to poor little Cinderella, she was also one twisted bitch. When Prince Charming comes a-knockin' with the glass slipper, in hopes of marrying off her butt-nasty daughters, the stepmother cuts off their toes and heels to try to get their gigantic feet into the delicate little shoes. The original story describes blood overflowing out of the shoe—what a lovely children's tale! So we knew that this woman was a mean old bitch—but who knew she was also originally written as something right out of a horror movie? Gee, I wonder why Disney left these details out of their cartoon version?

SURVIVAL TIP

THINK TWICE ABOUT ACCEPTING THAT JOB AT THE CEMETERY

THE QUIET IS NICE, BUT MY COWORKERS CAN GET DOWNRIGHT EVIL AT TIMES.

Just as one man's trash is another man's treasure, one girl's dream job is another chick's worst nightmare. But the truth is, everyone needs a paycheck and we can't always be picky. When you've been out of a job for a while, it's hard to stay discriminating when faced with eating Ramen noodles for the sixth night in a row. However, you gotta consider just how far you're willing to go for your job. You don't want to be the type who lives to work . . . and even more importantly, you do *not* want to be the type who dies for her job.

In the 1994 Italian horror flick, *Dellamorte Dellamore* (or *Cemetery Man*), poor Francesco has a job I wouldn't wish on my worst enemy. In addition to taking care of the headstones of the people buried at his cemetery, his main responsibility is rekilling the zombies who rise from their graves on the seventh day after their burials. Unable to convince his employers of what his job actually entails, he decides that it is less of a hassle to just take out the zombies. Eventually, Francesco becomes increasingly frustrated by his lack of options—and seems doomed to live out the rest of his life as the zombie killer.

If you find yourself faced with the prospect of a dead-end job like the cemetery man's, consider the pros and cons before accepting. Your coworkers could make day-to-day life a drag, it's hard to get vacation time, and when it comes time to look for another job, you'll have a damned hard time getting a recommendation.

 SCREAM QUEEN SAYS *Although it sounds like an interesting profession, you may find that it's just another dead-end job.*

SURVIVAL TIP

RUN FASTER THAN YOU BELIEVE TO BE NECESSARY

IT'S NOT THAT I'M NOT SCARED, BUT IT SEEMS RIDICULOUS TO RUN FROM SOMEONE WHO MOVES SO SLOWLY.

As long as there have been horror movies, there have been zombie movies. And every zombie movie has small but noticeable differences. In some movies, the zombies look like regular people, only with a slightly greenish tone to their skin. In others, the zombies look like Michael Jackson's backup dancers in *Thriller*, rotting and oozing with their pieces falling off whenever they move. But no matter how the zombies look, they all have this in common: they're never going to make the high school track team.

When you're watching a zombie movie, it seems ridiculous when the characters run away at top speed. *Idiots!* you laugh to yourself. *They're wasting all that energy running from someone who could never catch them in a million years!* The camera pans back to the zombies (who tend to travel in packs) who seem in no more of a rush to catch their prey than they are to iron their burial clothes and reattach their limbs. Instead, they amble along, moseying about as if they're window-shopping. They move so freaking slow, it's easy to forget that they're actually chasing someone. But what happens next is one of the biggest mysteries of the horror genre. Defying all reason, without showing any signs of speeding up, the zombies catch their victims, and it's a brain buffet.

Most horror fanatics agree that eventually, the dead will rise again (Wait, no. That's the Catholics—but you get the idea). And when they do, you may find yourself being chased by a group of rotters. True, it may seem like they'll never catch you—but learn from those poor suckers who ended up as zombie food. As laughable as it may seem, you gotta run like you've never run before. Don't stop running until you're in your car driving away from them, quickly. It may not be logical, but once zombies are attacking you, logic has pretty much gone out the window.

 SCREAM QUEEN SAYS Night of the Living Dead *actually appears to have been filmed entirely in slow motion.*

NEVER SAY NEVER UNTIL SOMEONE'S HEAD HAS BEEN SEVERED

I SHOT HIM! NOW I CAN ENJOY THE PEACE AND QUIET.

If you're a horror fan, you've seen a lot of people die in a lot of different ways. You've seen people shot, stabbed, axed, slashed, burned, bombed, and so on. In horror movies, there are almost as many ways to kill someone as there are chicks with big boobs and flashlights. This info might prove useful to you when battling evil people. But when battling the undead, you have to throw out almost all the rules you've learned about how to kill someone. When it comes to zombies, if movies like *Night of the Living Dead* and *Zombieland* have taught us anything, it's that those regular old methods of retaliation ain't gonna cut it. You can't stop until the zombie is in pieces.

There are few species whose genetic makeup dictates how they have to eat the big one. Everyone knows vampires need that stake through the heart. And most people are aware of the ol' silver bullet trick to take down werewolves. But few are aware of how ineffective efforts to off zombies can be if you're not willing to rip those disintegrating dudes into a dozen different parts. So consider yourself informed. If you're staring down an undead bastard, slow him down using one of the usual methods of wasting someone—and then grab your friend who has a strong stomach for gore, and together, hack your pursuer into as many pieces as you can stand. Then, grab a match. Only when you're roasting marshmallows over a burning zombie can you breathe that sigh of relief.

 SCREAM QUEEN SAYS *You might want to breathe through your mouth; I can't imagine roasted zombie smells as good as roasted weenies.*

MY BAD: F-UPS ON FILM: JENNIFER'S BODY

Demonic Jennifer in 2009's *Jennifer's Body* is one tough bitch. After being falsely assumed a virgin and offered up in a satanic sacrifice, Jennifer herself is demonized and can only be satisfied by eating human flesh. In one scene, a poor dude, thinking he's about to get lucky, ends up being torn limb from limb, and everything Jen was too full to finish is left behind for the animals. In a clear show of Discovery Channel ignorance, the movie depicts a deer eating Jennifer's leftovers. The f-up here is that deer are in fact vegetarians and wouldn't eat human remains. The image is inarguably creepy but scientifically inaccurate. No worries, though. It's a little known fact . . . and is far from the only wrong thing about this overall dud of a movie.

SURVIVAL TIP

IF A VIRUS IS TURNING THE PEOPLE IN YOUR TOWN INTO KILLING MACHINES, GET THE HELL OUT OF DODGE

EVERYONE HERE IS GETTING SICK AND THEN GOING CRAZY . . . I BETTER TRY TO HELP THEM BY DRINKING OUT OF THE SAME GLASS AND NOT WASHING MY HANDS AFTER I TOUCH THEM.

In horror movies, you've always gotta look out for number one. Anyone who tries to go for help (Remember *Stick with the Group*) or otherwise save a person or group from sure death usually finds herself in the crossfire. And whether the enemy is human, zombie, monster, demon, alien, or a *virus that turns people into zombies*, that rule doesn't change. If your city is under attack by a killer virus (or worse, a virus that makes people killers), don't try to save anyone—just take your as-of-yet uninfected ass and get the hell away from the host monkeys.

But! I can hear you whining, *what if I have to save my mom or my boyfriend or best friend who can't get away? Or* (and I can tell now you're really upset) *what if someone I love like my dad or my grandma or my brother already has the virus and I have to stay to make sure they don't get killed or locked up with the really sick and crazy people?* Here's some Scream Queen tough love for you: TFB. Leave 'em behind while you still have your health.

At the beginning of 1973's *The Crazies*, residents of a Pennsylvania town are beginning to act a bit, shall we say, fucking nuts. No one knows the cause behind the strange behavior, but it turns out that the aforementioned nuts have been stricken by a strange and contagious virus that is spreading through the water supply. Released when a plane carrying an untested bio weapon crashed, the poisonous virus is slowly spreading across the entire city. Not just any old cough or cold, this virus goes beyond sniffles and the runs—it causes the infected people to become murderous psychos. And if that wasn't enough of a problem, the National Guard gets involved and decides that the best way to take care of this little problem is to start killing people right and left.

The movie centers around a young couple, David and Judy, who in their respective jobs as a fireman and a nurse see firsthand some of the strange behavior that residents of Evans City are beginning to exhibit. Inexplicably, David is immune to the virus. Unfortunately, pregnant Judy has caught this little bug and is well on her way to becoming a total nutjob. With "the crazies" and the trigger-happy soldiers intent on killing everyone with a pulse, David is determined to save his baby's mama and her unborn child. Big mistake, David. Let's just say that this ending is far from happy.

⚠ In killer virus movies, there's always one character with unexplained immunity. If the murderous virus strikes your town and you happen to be the one safe from the killer germ, don't stick around to try to save everyone—make sure everything and everyone is destroyed. Will Smith's character stuck around in *I Am Legend*. David did in *The Crazies*. You know what these two have in common? Nothing. Except the fact that they're both dead. ⚠

 SCREAM QUEEN SAYS *Horror viruses make that H1N1 look like a cakewalk.*

SURVIVAL TIP

IF YOU'RE THE ONE HUMAN IMMUNE TO A VIRUS THAT CREATES ZOMBIES, KEEP THAT SECRET TO YOURSELF

I SWEAR I'M NOT IMMUNE TO THE ZOMBIE VIRUS! I JUST TAKE A LOT OF VITAMIN C!

We've already established the fact that in horror movies, when someone catches a virus, it usually goes beyond a runny nose and diarrhea. In movies such as *28 Days Later*, *28 Weeks Later*, and *I Am Legend*, it means that a person who catches the bug is going to end up a flesh-eating monster, determined to wipe out the very species that they used to belong to. In a race against time, the dwindling humans try to find a way to reverse the effect of the virus. And there's always one person who holds the key—the person who knows the secrets to becoming immune to the effects of the germ. Lucky guy, right? Well, sort of . . . if he can keep his secret to himself.

⚠ In *28 Weeks Later*, Alice is inexplicably immune to the illness that is turning the rest of Britain's population into psychotic, zombie-like murderers. Her genetic code provides the key for humans to regain control of the earth. Unfortunately, she's not around long enough to prove scientifically useful. God, those zombies are a vindictive bunch. ⚠

When it comes to surviving the zombie virus, if you have what it takes to remain immune, take a lesson from the herpes crowd and keep your little secret to yourself.

 SCREAM QUEEN SAYS *Like herpes, the anti-zombie virus is the gift that keeps on giving.*

SURVIVAL TIP

DON'T PERFORM RESEARCH ON A SPECIES CAPABLE OF REVENGE

I DON'T KNOW WHAT HE'S SO UPSET ABOUT. I ALWAYS KEPT HIS CAGE CLEAN AND THE EXPERIMENTS I PERFORMED ON HIS BODY WERE SCIENTIFICALLY GROUNDBREAKING!

We humans are not the most sensitive of species. You need only look to the rainforest or the ozone layer (okay, so those are both pretty far away, but you see what I'm saying) to realize that we're usually seeking immediate gratification and saying, "Oh, well" to the consequences. Our destruction of nature has had pretty harsh consequences so far (hello, global warming). But in horror movies, let's say that the penalties for such selfish thinking are far more immediate.

In 2007's *I Am Legend*, Will Smith plays Robert Neville, the planet's lone survivor of a horrible virus that turns people into alien-looking, people-eating, zombie guys, the result of an anti-cancer vaccine that, to put it lightly, went a bit awry.

The movie follows Neville going about his day with his German Shepherd, left to roam the streets of New York City on his own, gathering food and attempting to keep himself from going insane for lack of human contact. At night, though, things go from a bit lonely to well, really, really scary. The alien-zombie guys, who are deathly allergic to daylight (if you can call spontaneous combustion an allergy), come out of hiding to wreak havoc—and when the monsters are able to trace Neville to his home, no amount of protective armor over the doors and windows can keep them out, especially given that Neville has been performing experiments on one of their kind in his basement. In case you haven't seen this thriller/horror, I won't give away the ending. But let's just say that when it comes to the poor Fresh Prince, zombies just don't understand.

District 9 takes man's self-appointed belle of the ball crown to a significantly bigger scale. After a spaceship lands over Johannesburg, humans in South Africa round up the aliens (which they derogatorily refer to as "prawns") and inter them in deplorable conditions, killing and torturing dozens of them in the name of scientific and military interest. When one of the government researchers becomes infected with an alien virus that begins to transform him into a prawn, the tables are turned and he finds himself under the microscope—and the knife—of the very agency he used to work for. Talk about sweet revenge.

If you happen to find yourself going toe-to-toe with an alien life-form who makes no sign of trying to threaten you or your species, do yourself a favor and think before you begin poking and prodding him. If invasion movies have shown us anything, it's that the life-form humans have tortured won't be too sympathetic to us when it's their turn to play alpha dog.

SCREAM QUEEN SAYS *We'll see how much you like it when your limbs are the ones being dissected.*

NO TRESPASSING

EVEN THE UNDEAD ARE PROTECTIVE OF THEIR YARDS!

Let's be clear about one thing: demons, ghosts, people driven crazy by the deaths of their loved ones—even years before—do not like when you mess with their land. Whether it's walking on new grass seed, cutting through someone's abandoned lot, or building a condo on an ancient burial ground, they're a territorial bunch. Bottom line here: watch your step.

⚠ And then there's the queen of "stay off my land, even if I'm dead" movies, *Poltergeist*. Limboed souls whose graves were displaced by a suburban housing development communicate through the television set with a freaky-little-blond kid. The Freeling family is haunted and ultimately, and quite literally, thrown out of their home when The Beast decides he's not down with what's happened to the place where he and hundreds of others were laid to rest. Cut to hundreds of bodies flying out of the ground, and you have one of the scariest movies ever—all because some white people from California thought it was a-okay to plow over a bunch of headstones. Geesh. You'd think that after someone's dead he wouldn't care who inhabits his land. ⚠ The undead are like the PETA of ancient burial grounds—you see where they're coming from, but their methods still seem a bit extreme.

 SCREAM QUEEN SAYS *Research the history behind land before you break ground on a new mall.*

CHAPTER 10

POSSESSED—AND PISSED OFF ABOUT IT

A friend of the devil is a friend of yours? Not so much. Becoming one of the devil's pawns doesn't seem fun at all—at least not as it's played out onscreen. In addition to the fact that the whole time you're possessed, you're a total bitch on wheels, it's hard to look cute when you're spewing supernatural venom on a priest or writhing as a demon is dragged from your bod.

Here are some tips that should help to ensure that the only resident of your body is, well, you.

IF A GYPSY ASKS FOR A FAVOR, GIVE IT TO HER

SORRY, OLD WOMAN OF INFINITE WISDOM AND IMMEASURABLE POWER, I'D LOVE TO DO YOU A FAVOR BUT MY HANDS ARE TIED.

There are certain people you really shouldn't mess with: the guy in charge of your school loans. The cable guy, who has the power to gift you with three free months of HBO and Cinemax—or leave you with a clicker that doesn't allow you to watch anything above channel 100. And, in what should be a no-brainer, a gypsy who has the ability to put a curse on your head that could cut your life quite short.

In 2009's *Drag Me to Hell*, young and ambitious Christine is hoping to be promoted to the position of assistant manager at the bank where she works as a loan officer. Having just been told she must prove herself as a tough decision maker, in perhaps the most poorly timed loan application ever, Christine's very next customer is an elderly gypsy who requests a third extension on her mortgage. Determined to show her ability to be cutthroat, Christine denies the gypsy's request for a loan extension—and immediately suffers the consequences. In quick succession, the gypsy curses her, attacks her, and dies before Christine can even try to convince her to lift the curse.

⚠ Pursued by a dark demon spirit, Christine is doomed from the moment she more or less says, "tough luck" to the gypsy in need. You have to wonder just what the hell she was thinking. After all, what menial job could be worth pissing off someone who has the power to invoke a demon? The one positive here is that we can all learn a lesson from Christine. If someone with any form of supernatural power needs something from you, it's far beyond reason for you to turn her down. True, it can be annoying when you feel like you lack choices. But that feeling of sticking to your guns? It's not going to help you stay out of the ground when the earth opens up and, well, drags you to hell. ⚠

 SCREAM QUEEN SAYS *It's not much of a spoiler alert when the title of the movie is* Drag Me to Hell.

SURVIVAL TIP

BE WARY WHEN YOUR MAN SHOWS EVEN LESS EMOTION THAN USUAL

YOU NEVER DO THE DISHES, YOU'RE NOT INTERESTED IN SEX ANYMORE . . . ALL YOU WANT TO DO IS CREATE ALIEN CLONES OF EVERYONE . . . AND WATCH SPORTS CENTER.

Stereotype or not, we are the fairer sex. We're also better communicators, more emotional, and overall, just more tuned in than the half of the population who pees standing up. Every girl has stood in wonder as her boyfriend or husband watches football for eleven straight hours or plays Guitar Hero until his thumbs knot up. And every girl has resisted (or given into) the almost uncontrollable urge to reach across the table and smack her man in his face when she realizes he's watching TV over her shoulder during the middle of a romantic dinner. It's not their fault that they're so clueless. But they are. So when a guy seems a bit zoned out, it's hard to tell if it's because he's just being a dude . . . or if his body has been stolen by an alien force determined to take over the world.

In 1978's *Invasion of the Body Snatchers,* aliens are taking over the earth by stealing people's "shells" (their bodies), killing their "multiples" (the host), and masquerading as the people whose shells they've taken over. These pod people are lethargic and have an absent look in their eyes—in other words, they're like half of the population during any broadcast of *Monday Night Football*. The problem is, they won't stop until the entire human population has been wiped out and replaced by these pods.

Given that approximately 80 percent of the human population believes in aliens, you'd better be prepared for the day when things take an *Invasion of the Body Snatchers* twist. But how can you make sure you're wiping out an alien pod person and not your run-of-the-mill, unfeeling dude? Lucky for you, The Scream Queen is here to help.

THE SCREAM QUEEN'S GUIDE TO DECIPHERING BETWEEN A DROID AND A DUDE	
YOUR GUY IS PROBABLY JUST BEING A DUDE IF HE:	YOU MIGHT HAVE A DROID ON YOUR HANDS IF HE:
doesn't cry at your grandmother's funeral	doesn't cry while watching a documentary about the 1980 Miracle on Ice
forgets your third anniversary even though you're spending the weekend at a romantic B&B	doesn't notice when your anniversary gift to him is a Brazilian wax and a six-pack
fakes being sick to get out of your cousin's winter wedding in Wisconsin	goes to the wedding without bitching
doesn't say thank you when you clean his entire apartment without asking for his help	doesn't yell at you when you accidentally vacuum up the pile of dirt from Fenway Park he keeps on his bedside table

While it's not a foolproof system, you'll have to use your keen powers of observation to tell if your boyfriend or husband is being himself or if he has, in fact, had his body taken over by a body snatcher. When all else fails, you can always try the "wear nothing but his favorite sports jersey" trick. The pod guy will probably try to sleep with you whereas your boyfriend would just tell you to hang it back up before you get anything on it.

 SCREAM QUEEN SAYS *In many ways, guys are easier to get along with after their bodies have been taken over by killer aliens from outer space.*

SURVIVAL TIP

IS YOUR NEW HOUSE POSSESSED BY A SPIRIT THAT MAKES THE RESIDENTS GO MAD AND KILL EACH OTHER? KEEP MOVING.

I THINK YOU COULD DO A LOT WITH THIS MEAT LOCKER WHERE THE PREVIOUS OWNER USED TO KEEP HIS FAMILY MEMBERS.

When people are house hunting, they look for different things in a potential home. Some go for hardwood floors, some won't settle for anything less than two and a half baths, and still others base their decisions solely on the school district that the home falls in. Me? I'm not hard to please. I just ask that my next home isn't built upon a mass burial ground, owned by a man who murdered his entire family in or around the house, or otherwise the site of a ritualistic massacre.

Both the 1979 and the 2005 film versions of *The Amityville Horror,* based on the book of the same title by Jay Anson, follow a young couple, George and Kathy Lutz, as they buy a charming house in a ritzy area of Long Island for a deep discount—due to the fact that the previous owner murdered his mother, father, two brothers, and two sisters in the house. Fully aware of the house's past and determined to rid it of its bad energy, the Lutzes enlist the help of a priest to bless it and its new inhabitants. The priest tries unsuccessfully, and is ultimately driven mad. But is that enough to get the Lutzes to move out of their new digs? Of course not. The real estate opportunists needed to be further convinced by the haunting of their own toilet and blood dripping from the walls.

The Lutzes aren't the only people whose poor home-buying decisions have come back to, ahem, *haunt* them, but they are the most notable. Although we may shake our heads at the lengths they went to for frugality, we can thank them for this valuable survival method. When it comes to horror flicks and real-life real estate repulsion, one truth remains: the break you may get in your mortgage payment will not be worth it when your own house turns against you.

 SCREAM QUEEN SAYS *It's amazing what some people will overlook for crown molding.*

IF YOUR HOUSEHOLD ELECTRONICS START TO MALFUNCTION WITHOUT EXPLANATION, DUCK

A RUNAWAY FOOD PROCESSOR BLADE CAN BE A REAL PAIN IN THE NECK.

Anyone who has ever lost cable in the middle of the new *True Blood* or whose frozen margarita party was cut short because the blender crapped the bed knows how irritating problems with home appliances can be. But in dozens of horror movies, troubles with all things plug-in are way more than little annoyances—thanks to the demons who take over the appliances, making them electrically powered killing machines. If the plot of a particular horror flick involves a malicious spirit or demon on the loose, you can count on one thing: the church is going to protest the movie premiere, ruining E's coverage of the red carpet. Oh, and one more thing—the first time a character is home alone, using a power saw to slice bread or an electric carving knife to cut a brick of cheese, someone is going to be beheaded.

It usually starts with a slight twitch of a power cord, the clueless actress too busy talking on the phone or getting a snack out of the refrigerator to notice. Before you know it, a blade sharp enough to cut bone is flying at the jugular of the large-breasted character. And as quick as you can say "Slap Chop!," someone is discovering a headless corpse, surrounded by dozens of julienne vegetables and a seemingly endless pool of blood.

When watching a movie, we can always see the Death by Appliance coming. We're tipped off by several things: the electric spark that occurs when the demon inhabits the toaster, the twisting of the cord into the shape of a noose, the character alone in the kitchen, the creepy music, the zoom in on the appliance, the glistening sharpness of a stainless steel blade.

But in the moment, you may be distracted and miss the signs, leaving you spouting blood and down an appendage or two.

We saw an extreme example of this in 1986's *Maximum Overdrive*. Based on a short story by Stephen King, this creepy movie shows the horror that occurs when appliances all over the world come to life and become homicidal. Starting with a waitress who gets her hand hacked off by an electric knife to tractor trailer trucks with minds of their own and a taste for blood, this movie is enough to make you want to adapt an Amish lifestyle and rid yourself of all household appliances.

Think about it—maybe becoming Amish wouldn't be so bad. Toast your bread over a candle, cut your vegetables with a plastic knife, move to a house without a garbage disposal. It will be well worth it when you hear how someone else got her brains scrambled by an electric mixer.

 SCREAM QUEEN SAYS *You'll have a hard time selling that Cuisinart on eBay if you disclose that it's possessed by the spirit of an undead murderer.*

REAL LIFE HORROR: THE AMITYVILLE HORROR

Jay Anson's *The Amityville Horror* is based on a true story. George and Kathy Lutz moved into 112 Ocean Avenue on December 23, 1975—thirteen months after the murders had occurred at the same address. As Anson's book famously begins, twenty-eight days later they fled in terror—leaving all of their possessions behind to be retrieved by a mover after both the Lutzes and their children reported witnessing paranormal activity. Much debate over the validity of their story exists, although both Lutzes took—and passed—lie detector tests. Anyone who has seen or read *The Amityville Horror* cannot believe the story is true, because if it is, well, shit, they would be too scared to ever move into another house again.

I just have one question here. Is a haunted toilet covered by homeowner's insurance?

SAY "HELL NO" TO HYPNOSIS
YOU'RE GETTING VERY SLEEPY ...

Somewhere along the way, hypnotism lost its reputation as a dark art that leaves the human mind far too open for someone or something to swoop in and mess with your brain. It has become a party trick, a mainstay of bachelorette parties, causing young unsuspecting chicks to quack like a duck whenever they hear a bell ring, or pretend to give a BJ every time the hypnotist claps his hands together. People use hypnotism as a way to quit smoking, lose weight, sleep better . . . it's the cure-all for everything. But that doesn't mean we should rely on it to save our asses. In fact, it has the potential to get our asses in trouble.

In 1999's *Stir of Echoes*, an amateur hypnotist leaves Tom, played by Kevin Bacon, an open door to incoming signals and messages from those who aren't around—you know, dead people—to use as their regular method of communication. Even though Tom is actually receiving these communications for the greater good (as in, to catch a murderer), neither he nor his family knows that, and he becomes possessed by the spirit who is using him to communicate. In short, he begins acting like a total lunatic. His actions cause those guilty of the crime Tom is unwillingly solving to come after Tom, his family, and his entire neighborhood. In short, the shit hits the fan and in a big way—all because of some poorly executed hypnotism.

There are some things humans aren't supposed to mess with—and the inner workings of other people's minds is one of those things. When opening the mind through hypnosis, it's way too easy to leave the window open for other people, spirits, or things to sneak in and take over. So even though it's become part of the self-help industry and the girls-acting-slutty biz, it doesn't mean hypnosis is something you should mess with. In the best case scenario, you end up mimicking sex acts in front of twenty of your closest girlfriends from college as well as the rest of a packed bar. In the worst case scenario, you end up with a demon calling the shots in your brain—and they're not all as nice as the one who told the Baconator to keep digging until he found who or what he was looking for.

 SCREAM QUEEN SAYS *I wonder who has possession of Kevin Bacon's brain every time he gets his hair cut.*

DON'T BEFRIEND A PRIEST WHEN THERE'S AN EXORCISM ON THE HORIZON

YOU CAN SAY "OH MY GOD" ALL YOU WANT, BUT HE'S NOT GOING TO BE ABLE TO HELP YOU THIS TIME.

Catholic priests (well, the good ones anyway) have had more of their fair share of trouble in the last one hundred years or so. When not facing down public scandal or reading the same book over and over again, they're being hauled to people's houses, hospitals, and their own churches to drag the spirit of the devil out of people—most often, from the only demographic whose personalities might actually improve if Satan possesses them: teenage girls.

In 2005's *The Exorcism of Emily Rose* and the mother of all possession movies, 1973's *The Exorcist*, priests are called to perform exorcisms after all other attempts to free the girls from Satan's power have proven ineffective. Although things end better for one priest than the other (as in, only one is struck dead by the spirit leaving the young girl's body), both are shaken to the point where they're not going to be able to sing a joyful hymn about the light of God anytime soon. And in both cases, some of the people around them become collateral damage in the Holy War for the girls' souls. So if someone you know is in need of an exorcism, by all means, make the call to the priest and arrange for the procedure. But if you value your life, stay far away from the site of the whole soul cleansing. It's not quite as simple as throwing some holy water around, and there are bound to be injuries.

Whether you're religious or not, you have to admire the guys who are so secure in their faith that even the threat of the devil isn't enough to shake their beliefs—although when that green vomit lands on the priest's collar in *The Exorcist*, he doesn't look so sure of himself.

 SCREAM QUEEN SAYS *Somehow, I doubt this is what these guys had in mind when they took their vows.*

SURVIVAL TIP

QUESTION YOUR FRIEND'S INHUMAN STRENGTH

THOSE PILATES CLASSES ARE REALLY PAYING OFF!

A good friend knows her best bud's strengths and weaknesses. You know better than anyone that your best friend has an insane ability to figure out the exact sales price of a buy one, get one 75 percent off deal on any two pairs of flats. You're also painfully aware of her inability to find her way from her driveway to, well, anywhere. And you'd probably be the first one to raise an eyebrow if your BFF suddenly had the ability to throw grown men across the room or to break someone's hand just by looking at him. Hopefully, if that happened, you'd realize that your friend is not the one in control anymore.

In *Jennifer's Body*, good ol' Satan himself possesses the title character after a botched virginal sacrifice and Jennifer's best friend, Needy, is clued in to something not being quite right after Jennifer spews gallons of black projectile vomit right in front of her eyes. However, not every possession is that in your face, so to speak. One sure sign that Jennifer was possessed happened even before the spewing episode—she displayed a sudden bout of inhuman strength by sending Needy flying into the wall.

Most likely, you don't have many friends who boast the brute strength of a jilted demon. So if you notice that your friend is suddenly all too willing to try opening a stubborn jar of pickles or begins to throw around people much larger than herself, stay on your toes. Sudden strength may not be a sure sign of possession, but unless you want to wait until that river of black spew hits your face, it's the closest you're going to get.

 SCREAM QUEEN SAYS *Kickboxing class is not going to make anyone strong enough to rip out another person's rib cage . . . and then eat it.*

Conclusion

WILL THESE GIRLS EVER LEARN?

"THIS IS THE MOMENT WHEN THE SUPPOSEDLY DEAD KILLER COMES BACK TO LIFE, FOR ONE LAST SCARE."
~SCREAM

It's hard to imagine a time when you'll ever need the 108 survival tips that some of the best horror movies have taught us and that I've gathered into this book. But that doesn't mean these lessons won't ever come in handy. After all, I bet most of the chicks whose stories have graced these pages never thought they would need to know how to fight off a possessed food processor or live through a night of babysitting the son of Satan. But stranger things have happened, and starting now, there's no excuse for any badass chick like yourself to end up cuffed and stuffed in some axe-wielding psycho's basement.

True, it's unlikely that you'll end up battling a satanic demon or an escaped mental patient, or wiping your best friend's brain matter off your brand new boots. But one thing is for sure: it's better to be safe than cut into ribbons And even if you never use industrial-sized wrench to bash a murderer's head in, you're armed with the knowledge you need to show anyone who's boss.

After all, no one ever messed with the Scream Queen and got away with it.

MUST-SEE SCARY FLICKS

You'd better upgrade that Netflix account, my friend. Here are the movies you'll need to see for yourself to believe.

#

28 Days Later

28 Weeks Later

30 Days of Night

A

A Nightmare on Elm Street

The Abandoned

Alien

Alien Versus Predator

Alligator II

American Psycho

Amityville Horror, The

And Soon the Darkness

Antichrist

Arachnophobia

B

Babysitter Wanted

Battle Royale

Big Love

Blair Witch Project, The

Braindead

Buried Alive

C

Cabin Fever
Candyman
Carrie
Cemetery Man
Children of the Corn
Crazies, The
Critters

D

Darkness Falls
Daybreakers
Dead & Buried
Dead Ahead
Dead End
Deliverance
Descent, The
Detour
District 9
Drag Me to Hell
Duel

E

Evil Dead, The
Evil Dead II
Evil Woods, The
Exorcism of Emily Rose, The
Exorcist, The

F

Faculty, The
Fatal Attraction
Feast
Final, The
Final Destination I and II
Firestarter
Frailty
Friday the 13th, The Final Chapter

G

Ginger Snaps
Gingerdead Man, The
Godfather, The
Good Son, The
Grudge, The

H

Halloween I, II, III, and IV, and Halloween H2O
Hand that Rocks the Cradle, The
Hills Have Eyes, The
Hitcher, The
Hostel
House of 1000 Corpses
House of the Dead
House of Wax

I

I Am Legend
I Know What You Did Last Summer
Invasion of the Body Snatchers
It

J

Jaws
Jeepers Creepers
Jennifer's Body
Jersey Shore: The Movie
Joy Ride: Dead Ahead
Just Before Dawn

K

Killer Movie

L

Lake Placid
Last House on the Left
Leprechaun
Long Weekend

M

Magic
Maximum Overdrive
May
Mist, The
My Girl

N

Night of the Living Dead

O

Omen I, II, and III, The
One Missed Call
Open Water
Open Water 2
Orphan

P

P2
Pee Wee's Big Adventure
Pet Semetary
Poltergeist
Prom Night
Prom Queen
Prophecy
Psycho

Q

Quarantine

R

Rest Stop
Ring, The
Ringu
Roadgames
Rosemary's Baby
Ruins, The

S

Saw

Saw V

Scary Movie

Scream

Scream 3

Se7en

Shaun of the Dead

Shining, The

Signal, The

Signs

Silence of the Lambs, The

Silent Hill

Single White Female

Slaughter High

Sleep Away Camp

Sleeping with the Enemy

Slumber Party Massacre, The

Stepfather, The

Stir of Echoes

Strangers, The

Summer of Sam

T

Texas Chainsaw Massacre, The

Thing, The

Thinner

True Blood

Turistas

Twilight

U

V

W

INDEX

Meredith O'Hayre grew up on the South Shore of Massachusetts and was never allowed to rent any horror movies for fear
she would try out some of the killer's moves on her younger
brother. The fears were not unjustified.

She became addicted to scary movies after watching *The
Shining* in an empty beach house in North Carolina while
on vacation with her family and hasn't looked back since.
O'Hayre earned her BA in English from UMass Amherst and
now lives with her scaredy-cat boyfriend back on the South
Shore, down the road from her badass nephew, sarcastically
lovable brother, and adoring parents. Talk about scary.

Find her on Twitter @SQSurvivalGuide.